Common Sense

Changing the Conversation of Life

Jeff Sangster

ISBN 978-1-64492-237-8 (paperback)
ISBN 978-1-64515-361-0 (hardcover)
ISBN 978-1-64492-238-5 (digital)

Christian Faith Publishing, Inc.
832 Park Avenue
Meadville, PA 16335
www.christianfaithpublishing.com

Original art by Bill Shurtliff

Printed in the United States of America

A long habit of not thinking a thing wrong, gives it a superficial appearance of being right... Time makes more converts than reason.

—Introduction to "Common Sense,"
Thomas Paine, 1776

Contents

Preface

The Conversation of Life

Abortion. Make no doubt about it, it's difficult to talk about. To tell the truth, abortion was one conversation I always did my best to avoid. Extreme emotions from the fringes of the issue have created a discussion so charged with feelings and emotion that it seems every conversation is more of a confrontation. As for me, I'm a straight down-the-middle kind of guy; be friendly, don't rock the boat, and gain no enemies. Avoiding any kind of discussion about abortion, and likewise any confrontation, was always priority one.

This is not to say, though, that I never thought about the abortion issue, or never considered to offer my opinion. There were certain times when I *wanted* to talk about abortion. There were other times when I thought that I *should* say something about abortion. But I didn't. I didn't want the fight. I didn't want to get involved.

So instead, I said nothing. If abortion ever came up, I just nodded my head, smiled, and then—

Changed the subject.

*****

Today's abortion debate is driven by a conversation that describes and defines for us the pictures of unborn human life and

7

abortion we see in our minds today. The words used by each side in this conversation paint very different pictures of unborn human life, and therefore define very different realities of abortion; yet each side claims to paint the truth.

All that we really need to do, we are told, is decide how we *feel* about what is presented to us and pick the picture we wish to see.

What do you see when you think of the abortion issue? Do you picture a political battle? The fight for women's freedom, reproductive rights, and right to privacy? The constitutional right of a woman to choose what she believes is best for her health and her body? Or do you picture a living unborn baby, and the fight to protect this life within the law? That abortion is nothing but the indiscriminate killing of an unborn baby? Maybe you don't know what to think, haven't paid much attention or simply don't care, and therefore have chosen to be somewhere within the middle.

Wherever you are on the abortion issue, this conversation has been the influence that has placed you there. This conversation, both the fuel and the fire of the abortion debate is, *the conversation of life.*

*****

The dominant voices of today's conversation are of the pro-choice/pro-abortion message. This message is channeled politically through the Democrat Party, and broadcast throughout society via the majority of mainstream popular media outlets; this including most Hollywood productions, network news channels, magazines, newspapers, and of course all forms of liberal social media. These voices adamantly dismiss any notion that an unborn baby is alive at any time within the womb of its mother and thereby focuses squarely on promoting and protecting the current constitutional freedoms granted to women concerning abortion. *Pro-Choice = Pro-Freedom. My body, my rights. Keep your religion out of my bedroom.*

The foundation for the pro-abortion argument is founded on the presumption that there *is no* objectively determined time during pregnancy when an unborn baby ever becomes *alive.* Instead, the reality of an unborn human life is believed and promoted to be only a *potential* life; that is maybe alive, maybe at some point, depending on what one might *believe,* but nobody can tell when for sure. And since the reality of existing life and humanity within the womb is only potential; that is, *subjective* to one's personal feelings, any moral values attached to this potential life can also only be determined subjectively; that is, by one's (specifically the pregnant woman's) individual interpretation regarding the existence of unborn life, and their (her) associated moral code toward this potential life and abortion. In other words, when a woman becomes pregnant, she has the individual right to decide whether the unborn baby she is carrying is alive, whether an abortion will kill her unborn baby, or whether this question of life or death even matters in accordance with her personal health and her choice to have an abortion. It's all part of a woman's choice. It's her right to choose.

Once the pro-abortion message is understood, the promotion of pro-abortion thought becomes easily recognizable in today's conversation, where the body issues, mental burdens, social inconveniences, societal placement, and financial concerns of a pregnant woman all take precedence over the care, well-being, and *potential life* of the unborn baby.

On the other side of the issue, filtering through the cracks of the popular media, are the softer pro-life voices, primarily reflected throughout society in some church theologies, one's personal moral values, and the political platform of the Republican Party. From the pro-life side, we hear words like *life, love,* and *responsibility*; and phrases like "life begins at conception," "it's a child, not a choice," and "if it's not a baby, you aren't pregnant." We hear that abortion *is* wrong because there *is* a living unborn baby involved, and that this baby *is* killed through an abortion procedure. Pro-life voices argue that the unborn baby is alive from the moment of conception, and that there are *severe* and *absolute* moral consequences involved with the legality of abortion in America. The pro-life message even goes as far as to contend that all forms of abortion are automatically and without exception morally wrong, even in situations of incest or rape, as these unborn children are living human babies as well, and therefore also entitled to the full protection of life under the law.

In today's conversation of life, voices of the pro-life movement are constantly attacked by the pro-abortion media for being on the wrong side of the conversation. The dominant pro-abortion media portrays the pro-life claim that unborn human life exists from the moment of conception not as any kind of truth, but instead as nothing more than one's mistaken personal belief, wayward individual philosophy, or religious fabrication of thought. "Keep your religion off my body." "Science is real, your beliefs aren't." "If you don't like abortion, don't have one." "Stop the war on women." Pro-life voices are regarded through the popular media as misguided philosophers of unborn life, right-wing political wackos, or wicked religious zealots; nothing but a small minority of foolish souls whose only goal is to force their mistaken religious morality and/or personal values down the throats of all American women. Pro-life attempts to promote any kind of moral and interior values opposing abortion, are quickly suppressed and deemed out of touch with the real values and needs of today's modern woman. Their close-minded, mean-spirited, and draconian "anti-rights," "anti-abortion," and "anti-women" mindset and protests are met by the pro-abortion media with aggravation, insensitivity, anger, and censor. Any foolish pro-life stand against abortion, the popular media infers, is based on nothing but philosophical, or theological, crock.

Then there is the middle ground, those who feel most comfortable in not taking a stand on the issue. There are a great many voices to this middle ground, but the general attitude is that there are more important issues to deal with, and better things to do, than bother with the abortion issue. Although the vast majority of those in the middle have ultimately turned a blind eye to abortion, they do at the same time generally accept the current abortion laws as they stand, and loudly voice their opposition to, the opposition of, abortion accordingly.

*****

I wrote this book as a conversation on today's conversation of life. Although I start this conversation by telling you a little more about me, and about how today's conversation of life influenced my attitudes and actions toward abortion, this book is not about me or my experiences. I simply use my experiences to point to a reflection, or a picture so to speak, of the current conversation of life in America. Then, together, we'll take a deeper look to see if this picture reflects the reality and truth of the abortion issue.

Even though I begin this book with my experiences, this book is not about what I *feel* to be true, or what I *believe* to be *real* about abortion. In the end, this book is purely about the facts. Through this conversation, we are out to find the truth; we are out to discover *what is* and *what isn't* unborn life and abortion in America.

I'm ready to talk…let's get started.

About Ignorance

The Lack of Knowledge, Education, or Awareness

I was only five when the US Supreme Court ruled in Roe v. Wade that women had the constitutional right to end a pregnancy through abortion. As you might think, I was too young to know anything about the issue, or much care. Growing up in a post-abortion world, I must not have paid too much attention to the issue because abortion meant nothing to me. The popular media's portrayal of the abortion issue—its "pro-choice" woman's rights rallies, or religious "anti-abortion" protests—were nowhere on my radar.

In fact, it wasn't until high school that I first remember hearing, or at least acknowledging, the word *abortion*. It was in the tenth grade, I was out with a group of friends on school lunch break, eating burgers and fries, talking about girls. One of my friends signaled aloud that he had a great story we just had to hear. The conversation went something like this.

"So, like, you know my buddy Dave? Well, he was dating this super-hot redhead from another school, great-looking girl. But you know, they got into this huge fight after he caught her talking to some other guy at a school dance. So anyway, they broke up a month or so ago." My friend leaned forward and lowered his voice. "So, like, this old girlfriend of his called him a couple of weeks ago and told him that she was—you know—late."

We all just sat there, our faces blank.

"She was pregnant!" he boomed. "What are you, a bunch of idiots?"

We all just sat there, our faces still blank.

My friend sat up big and tall, puffed out his chest and raised his voice. "So Dave's, like, telling this girl, 'There's no way you're pregnant with my baby. Get out of here, you're nothing but a stupid whore. How do I know who you've been with? You'd better not have told anybody."

He settled down, finished off his burger, and hushed his voice again. "So, like, this redhead told him like a thousand times that she was a hundred percent certain that 'it' was his, but he didn't have to worry because she hadn't told anyone, yet."

My friend paused for a moment, then grinned. "So she told him that she wanted to get *an abortion*, but she didn't have the money to pay for it." He sat up and stuffed a handful of french fries into his mouth. "Dave's like totally broke, so he borrowed money from everyone he knew. Heck, I even gave him fifteen bucks." He grabbed his pop and took a good, long drink from the straw until there was nothing left but ice and air. "So anyway, I gave him a little money to help him—you know—make bail!" He giggled and shifted back and forth in his seat.

Once again, we just sat there, our faces as blank as before.

"You guys are a bunch of idiots! I gave him some money so he could give this wench the hundred and fifty bucks she needed to have the abortion. You know, to 'take care of it.'"

He stopped there, looked to the ceiling and then gave a loud, long, belch.

"Here's the kicker. She was never pregnant!" He laughed big and out loud. "Can you believe it? She was never pregnant!" He stood up, signaling that it was time for us to get back to school. "But she's a smart one, and she took him for a hundred and fifty bucks!"

Finally, the punch line hit us, and we broke into a quick laugh. "No way man. That's just wild. She set him up big-time." The rest of us got up to leave. "Hey man, your friend Dave is an idiot."

My buddy opened the door and held it for everyone. "So do you think I should ask him for my fifteen bucks back?" He didn't stop laughing until we got to the car.

*****

That was it, my first encounter with abortion. Just a matter-of-fact, everyday part of high-school life, the backdrop to a practical joke. I pictured through the context of the story that *an abortion* somehow stopped the pregnancy from continuing, or otherwise did something to make a girl not pregnant anymore.

I was fifteen years old, abortion was new to me, and I knew nothing about it. Nobody had ever taken the time to teach me anything about abortion—not at home, not in school, not at church—and by the time I finished high school, nothing changed. Through my high-school years, what I would come to understand about the issue originated in the themes of teen-driven movies and the various coverages of abortion by the popular media. "No real harm ever comes to the baby during an abortion." "The baby isn't human, it isn't alive." "Abortion saves girls from the problem of being pregnant. Guys benefit from abortion too." "It isn't about a baby; it's about the rights of the mother." I gained some additional perspectives through the passing comments or off-handed jokes of my friends, and the blanks I simply filled in with my own personal thoughts and perceptions.

What I ended up painting for myself was a vague picture of abortion, with no real definitions of *anything*. I saw abortion as nothing but a last-ditch chance for a girl who had gotten pregnant to simply cancel her pregnancy. As for the abortion procedure itself, I guessed that it somehow stopped a pregnancy from continuing past a point of no return; but I didn't know how, or why. To me, abortion simply put a stop to what I considered as some kind of potential pregnancy, before a *real* baby was formed, before it would be considered a *real* pregnancy.

And what about later, what happened to the unborn baby if a woman had an abortion late in her pregnancy? Honestly, I didn't think women could have an abortion late in a pregnancy.

For the simple fact that abortion is a legal right for women in America, I reasoned that there couldn't possibly be any real harm to an unborn baby, except for the fact that it would never be able to grow enough to be born. "Abortion doesn't kill the baby, it just stops the pregnancy." It was easy for me to believe that all that unborn life stuff had to have been considered by doctors, lawyers, and lawmakers much smarter than me before abortion ever became legalized in America. There had to be good reasons why abortion was legal, real medical reasons why the unborn baby wasn't harmed or killed. Again, my best guess was that there was some sort of grace period that allowed enough time for a girl to have an abortion before there were any major consequences for the unborn baby, a grace period known by medicine and science, built in by nature.

Again, I didn't know, but neither did I ever care to give it much thought.

But if a girl did get pregnant, I knew plenty of reasons why she would want to have an abortion. The convenience, practicality, and economy of abortion is so widely broadcast across society through the pro-abortion media, who can miss it? Being a teenager, I thought it was all about hiding the truth—not only hiding a pregnancy, but unapproved sexual activity as well. Teen movies built up abortion as a savior for teen girls portrayed as too young and immature to have a baby and become moms, or as the only way of avoiding the wrath of out-of-touch, overly conservative parents, or society itself. Boyfriends embraced abortions for the same reasons. Some media outlets claimed it was all about the beauty of a woman's body, and her right to keep pregnancy from ruining it. Others focused on girls making mistakes, bad choices, and the negative stigma of being pregnant or other social inconveniences. Some claimed financial issues, of having to place a career on hold, or the added expense of adding a child to the family. Body issues, mental burdens, careers, relationships, societal issues, financial concerns, and sexual freedom all added fuel to the argument as to why abortion was good for women.

We are constantly told that abortion is the best way to fix a woman's *problem* of having an unplanned or unwanted pregnancy: "Get an abortion. Pregnancy over. Problems solved." After having an abortion, a woman can go on through life as though her pregnancy never existed. No one has to know, no one has to see it, no one has to talk about it. There would be no baby, no issues of pregnancy, and no responsibilities of parenthood. Girls, as well as guys, can do as they please, be as sexually free as they wish. Abortion is always there for them, the perfect alibi, the friend that would always be there to cover their story.

*****

That was it, my high school reality of abortion, the picture I had painted for myself as a teen. My picture was a confused, blurry, and abstract portrait painted through the primary influences of today's abortion conversation. No, I didn't know a whole lot about abortion. To me, it was just another teenage mystery, another "girl thing" I didn't really understand, nothing more than an everyday thing that a girl could just *do* if she wanted to, like get a tattoo, pierce her ears, or get a weird haircut.

Although I didn't care much about the abortion issue, deep inside, it made me uneasy. Even with all the positive promotion of abortion, I was uncomfortable with the idea of stopping a pregnancy through an abortion. But I couldn't explain why. It was just how I felt, deep inside. But there was no way I was going to move my position to the other side, the "wrong" pro-life side, and be subject to all that fire and criticism. No, I just kept my feelings to myself. I also thought it odd that for such a loudly touted right, women who had abortions were very quiet about it. It just seemed that if a girl did have an abortion, it was always done on the sly, behind somebody's back, in the darkness and shadows of life. If it were truly the right thing to do, I figured women would be more open about it.

This put me smack dab in the middle of the abortion issue. I knew of abortion only from what I saw around me, and what I saw didn't fully agree with how I felt inside. But I didn't know why. I was clueless about abortion and unborn human life, and without knowing any reasons to care either way, I did my best to step aside from the issue and stay clear of the conversation. I didn't know, or want, the fight. I learned early on that should abortion ever come up, it was much easier to just nod my head, smile, and then—

Change the subject.

*****

Looking in from the outside, many abortion conversations start out in an innocent and unassuming manner: a simple statement relating to abortion, or one's personal viewpoint toward women's rights, or maybe a perspective toward unborn human life. Sometimes, after a quick, countering reply, a mutual truce is somehow assumed between the two parties, and the conversation will seamlessly move on to a more pleasant, less controversial topic. Many times, however, this doesn't happen, at which point it might be best to duck-and-cover, for that initial skirmish is well on its way to a full-blown confrontation, complete with volley after volley of attack and counterattack, each filled with plenty of implied insult and injury.

I remember the first time I saw just such a confrontation, one in which I became a reluctant participant.

It was in my early college years, in an introductory biology class. My lab group had just finished cleaning up a small mess from an experiment we had just completed when we—meaning they, the others in my group—began to examine and discuss the results of the experiment. I was on the outside of this conversation, nothing more than an uninvolved bystander, lost in a world of my own. Somehow, while I was off in never-never land, the topic of conversation turned to abortion. Once I came to and realized what was going on, I made an instinctive attempt to change the subject. But it didn't work. This conversation had a life of its own and it was getting heated. I wanted nothing more than to shrink down within myself, become invisible, and stay out of it.

There was a lone voice at the center of this conversation: a girl's voice, a beautiful girl's voice. I will never forget her. She was radiant: rich dark hair, a great smile, deep blue eyes, and a calm, soothing way of speaking. But there was something more to her, a loveliness that I couldn't quite place; one that transcended anything in the physical.

She possessed a softness, a kindness, a love; an intangible beauty that seemed to radiate from the inside out. I had never sensed this in anyone before. The power of this intangible love, her undefined beauty, captivated me.

She stood all alone at the center of this conversation, defending her stance on abortion—*her pro-life stance*. I had never, ever seen anything like this before: a girl my age, standing up *against* abortion. I could hardly believe it.

Her actions were a lesson in grace. Speaking from that special beauty deep inside, she purposely, yet compassionately, conveyed her pro-life reasoning against the judgments, accusations, and personal attacks of her classmates. She was under constant fire, yet calmly stood her ground, that inner beauty showing front and center, as if to protect her from the insults that were being flung her way. Her defense of the unborn baby was more than just courageous—it was beautiful. It was love.

As I sat there watching this spectacle, she became more beautiful and lovely by the minute. My feelings for her soared with every word she spoke. She was so calm, so pretty, her words so loving, and her bravery against the attacks of her classmates nothing but incredible. I could hardly believe that this girl, so soft and so beautiful, would involve herself in a conversation like this—especially on the pro-life side, the wrong side of the conversation.

She never once wavered from her position.

I, on the other hand, had swapped sides multiple times.

Yet, no matter which side I happened to be on at the time, I still couldn't take my eyes off her. I was hopelessly lost in a vision of love. Then, from out of the blue, this beautiful girl turned, looked me square in the eyes, and asked, "What do you think, Jeff?"

I froze. A bolt of electricity immediately exploded up my back. I tried to look away, but I couldn't. Her eyes held mine fixed. Her gaze drove straight through me, deep into my soul. I could feel the intense energy of her brilliant blue eyes penetrate deep into my brain, probing the dark recesses of my mind, searching for an intelligent answer to her question.

I highly doubt she found anything.

Make no mistake about it, deep inside I was giddy—if not shocked—that this beautiful girl would utter a spoken word in my direction. But I was completely out of my element in this conversation. To make matters worse, she wanted me to tell her my feelings on abortion—something that I not only didn't know anything about, but couldn't have cared any less about as well.

Thoughts about what to do bolted back and forth across my mind. She wanted me to pick a side. No, she wanted me to pick *her* side. And I wanted to, I wanted to join her and be a part of that intangible beauty, that love. But I couldn't; there was no way. I was uncomfortable with a girl having an abortion, but I had no idea how to explain why and there was no way I was going to be subject to the attacks of my classmates. I probably could've latched onto her arguments, only I wasn't listening to what she was saying. Even though I didn't necessarily think abortion was a good thing, I always stood more or less in the middle of the issue. But being in the middle and agreeable to both sides of the abortion issue is one thing; choosing a side, especially *her* pro-life side, and then having to explain why to an otherwise hostile crowd, is another.

But I wasn't going to blow this chance to make a good impression on this girl. After quickly gathering some resemblance of composure, I did what any guy in my position would have done. I improvised. I shot from the hip. Right then and there, I came up with my first official positions toward abortion. I acted quickly, using a formula with which I was very familiar: stay smack dab in the middle, be friendly, don't rock the boat, and gain no enemies.

I drew a deep breath. I was between a rock and a hard place. I really wanted to impress this girl and say something that she wanted to hear, yet at the same time I didn't want to get involved in the confrontation.

Slowly I exhaled, and what stuttered out went something like this: "Well, I personally wouldn't make a girl have an abortion…if I were a girl, I wouldn't have an abortion…I don't think it's a good idea. What if there really *is* a baby inside?"

I was confident that that beautiful girl would like what just staggered out of my mouth. A calming sense of relief came over me;

that is, until I glanced up—and saw nothing but glares from the others coming in my direction. That was all it took. I caved. "But you know, I think that if a girl wants to have an abortion, she can go right ahead. It's her life, not mine… That isn't my decision to make, seeing as I am a guy, you know…"

I looked down, pretending to jot down some notes on the experiment, signaling that I was done talking.

And there it was, out of the clear blue sky, without knowing anything about the realities of unborn life, or what actually happens during an abortion procedure, I came up with my very own personal talking points toward abortion: *I didn't necessarily think that abortion was a good thing, but if a girl wanted to have one, it's legal, so who am I to stop her?*

These voiced opinions were based on the uneasiness toward abortion I felt deep inside, combined with the perceptions of abortion and unborn life formed by the pro-abortion media throughout my high school days. These opinions would go on to form my perspectives, attitudes and actions toward abortion for years to come.

Overall, I was happy with what I said. For the first time in my life, I had a stance on abortion to, well, stand on. It didn't matter to me that I was firmly entrenched in the middle. The important part was that I didn't make any waves or have to further explain my statements. Yes, I liked my newly cemented positions on abortion. They were easy to say and easy to defend. They were the best of both worlds, very much acceptable and not confrontational. I stayed in the middle, I was friendly, I didn't rock the boat, and I gained no enemies.

Unfortunately for me, though, I don't think that beautiful girl was very impressed with what I said.

Well, you win some, you lose some. Life goes on. Anyway, I didn't think it mattered one way or the other what I thought or said about abortion. My opinion, even if I came out against abortion, wasn't going to change anything. The abortion issue was way bigger than I was. Besides, abortion wasn't even in my realm of life; it was something that only other guys had to consider. Not me. I figured that the odds of me ever having to personally deal with the abortion issue were—incredibly slim.

About Inadequacy

Not Being Good Enough for an Intended Purpose

A short while later, I received a phone call from a good friend's younger sister. It was a nice surprise to hear from her. We had been friends since we were kids and I hadn't talked to her since she went off to college.

I'd always liked this girl. She was fun to be around: pretty, smart, outgoing and bubbly; her personality full of life. But talking with her this time on the phone, I could tell something was up, something was wrong in this conversation. She wasn't herself. She seemed to be troubled, her sentences were short and guarded, her voice strained, shaky, and out of sorts. Most of the time she rambled on as if she wanted to tell me something, yet at the same time, she seemed to be doing her best to avoid it. Soon enough, the words she needed to say, but didn't want to say, sounded through the receiver.

"I'm pregnant," I could tell from her voice that she was holding back tears, "and I don't know what to do."

"Okay—"

That was about all I could come up with.

For the next half hour or so she went on, detailing her situation, explaining the hows and whys, the thens and nows. She was in college, pregnant, and on her own. Her boyfriend was gone, he left her when she told him she was pregnant. She was lost. She wanted me to come visit her. She wanted me to help her think everything over. She needed an uninvolved opinion, an objective voice to help her decide what to do.

"I'm scared," she said.

I told her I'd be there in a couple of hours.

There I was, right smack dab in the middle of another conversation of life. Only this time, it was real life.

It was dark and rainy when I got into my car and left to see her. Thinking about her situation on my way there, I wasn't sure what I was going to say, or how I was going to help. Initially, I figured I would just rely on my then, well-honed comments and opinions toward abortion and unborn life, my middle-of-the-road positions first reached that one day in college biology class. But I wasn't sure if this was going to help. Middle-of-the-road was not going to work in her situation. She would need real answers to real questions—real questions that unfortunately, I had no answers for.

For the first time in my life, I wished I knew more about unborn human life and abortion. I wished I knew what actually happened when a girl had an abortion.

I was still uncomfortable with the idea of a girl having an abortion, but I still couldn't explain why. I'd heard the pro-life voices claiming that an unborn baby was alive from conception, I'd heard them talk about how this baby was killed during an abortion procedure. But these standpoints were adamantly attacked and dismissed throughout the rest of society. *How could they be so right,* I thought, *when so many adamantly argue that they are so wrong?*

I figured she would have real questions about abortion and doubts about pregnancy—probably the same questions and doubts that I had. Questions about pregnancy, an unborn baby, and abortion littered my thoughts. For the first time in my life, I truly wondered, *What is an abortion anyway? What actually happens? What do they do?* I figured that something that could grow into a baby had to be removed from the mother during an abortion, but just what was that something? *Could it be a real baby? Was it alive? Was it really just a glob of tissue and blood like they say?*

After contemplating these questions for a while, I began to reason with myself. *If something is removed during an abortion, it prob-*

ably isn't anything yet, can't be, definitely can't be anything real. Maybe they just inject something that makes whatever it is stop growing, and then it just goes away.

I eventually convinced myself that it really didn't matter what happened during an abortion, or even if a real baby was involved. That wasn't why she called. She wanted me to help her decide either to stay pregnant and have the baby, or have an abortion to end the pregnancy. It would be one or the other. The question was, which one she would choose.

Which one would she choose? That I didn't know. I didn't get a feel from her on the phone which way she was leaning.

I knew which way I wanted her to go. Deep inside I thought it would be best if she stayed pregnant and had the baby. At least, that is what my gut instincts told me. I had always said that I wouldn't make a girl have an abortion, and if I were a girl, I was sure that I would stay pregnant and have the baby as well. *But why? Why did I think it would be better for her to have the baby instead of an abortion? Why did I think having the baby was the right thing to do?* I was stuck. I didn't have any slam dunk reasons against having an abortion other than that to me, it just didn't seem right.

Her staying pregnant and having the baby would be the easiest for me to deal with for sure. I couldn't even remotely imagine how drastically this would change her life, but it still felt like it was the right thing to do. *But what if she didn't want to have the baby, or wasn't sure? Then what would I do? What if she really wants to have an abortion? What was I to do then?* A large void formed in my thoughts and confusion set in. I knew that I didn't believe enough in my own feelings to convince her otherwise. Trying to justify for my friend, the decision to not have an abortion, to stay pregnant and have the baby, suddenly became an awfully big proposition.

Then I began to wonder if I should even try. Maybe she should just make up her own mind. *What if she really just wants to have an abortion, and she just wants my support? What if she decides to have one anyway? Am I okay with that? Does it matter that much to me?* I didn't know. *Does it make sense to even try to influence her decision? Maybe I should just support her and whatever decision she decides to make.*

The more I pondered, the more I justified a position from which to work. I just reverted to my earliest ideas of abortion. *It isn't a big deal if she wants to have an abortion; it's just a last-ditch effort to not be pregnant. If she doesn't want to become a mom, she could just cancel the pregnancy, give the baby back. There has to be some kind of grace period. An abortion simply shuts off the pregnancy, like it never happened.* My thoughts began to clear.

I concluded that she would simply have to decide for herself if she wanted to have a baby and be a mom. *And if she wants to have the baby?* That's great; she could always place it up for adoption if she felt she couldn't handle caring for it. *And if she decided to have an abortion?* Although it didn't feel right to me, that would be her decision, and I guess I would have to be okay with that as well. She could just have an abortion. Pregnancy over, troubles solved. If that is what she wanted to do, then that's what she should do.

It was as simple as that. I would support her from the middle and not stand in the way of either decision. This wasn't going to be as difficult as I originally thought. It all boiled down to what I thought would be a relatively simple decision: either stay pregnant and have a baby, or get an abortion. All she had to do was make this decision by herself, for herself. This was nothing but a choice, her choice.

My mind eased.

*****

It was pitch-dark when I arrived at her building, the rain cold and drenching. Walking up the steps to her apartment, I felt confident that I could somehow help her, and be there for her. But when my friend answered the door, the confusion returned. Her face showed everything—the fear, the anxiety, the pain of indecision. She let me in and shut the door. I took off my jacket, shook the water off, and threw it on a nearby chair. By the time I turned to face her, she was already crying.

I took a deep breath. This was going to be difficult.

We sat and talked at the kitchen table for quite a while. I pretended to be calm and collected, and to be strong for her. But her situation was difficult and much more complicated than I imagined. She felt as though the whole world had come against her.

The more she talked, the more my insides twisted. It was clear that there was far more pressure from those around her to have the abortion. Her friends all tried to help by offering different versions of the same advice: that having an abortion would be the right thing to do to take care of her *problem* of being pregnant. Her ex-boyfriend made his feelings clear through curse words and threats. I wasn't at all surprised to find that her family didn't know she was pregnant.

My friend was a nervous wreck: anxious, tired, and confused. But even through all of the anxiety and fatigue, something else somehow found a way to radiate out from deep within her, a conflicting signal of sorts, one that looked to oppose the advice of her friends. It's hard to explain what it might have been, an emotion, or instinct maybe. But whatever it was, I could tell it was there. It seemed that deep down inside, she didn't like what her friends were telling her to do: she didn't want to have an abortion, that she *wanted* to have the baby. From deep inside, it seemed that all she wanted, all she needed, was for someone to tell her that everything would be okay, that nothing was really wrong, and there were good reasons to have the baby; and that they would help show her how.

Maybe that's why she called me. But I knew that person couldn't be me; I didn't have a clue.

I could see this gut intuition within her twisting and wrenching with her thoughts and emotions for no other reason than it went completely against the intense pressure and influences from everyone around her to simply have an abortion, to end her pregnancy. It was as if her most inner feelings, her inner thoughts and emotions, were being pulled from two different directions: one from the inside, the other from the outside.

I didn't help much.

When the talking was over, she finally asked, "What do you think I should do?"

An uneasy feeling settled in my stomach. "Well, if I were the dad, I wouldn't make you have an abortion. I don't think abortion is a good idea. I think you should have the baby. You can handle it, I think you are strong enough. But in the end, it's your choice, I can't tell you what to do. This is your decision, but whatever you choose, I'll be here for you either way."

Sitting at the table with her that night, these statements were the easiest to say. Yet at the same time, they were the hardest to say. I was caught in the middle of a situation that was way more than I had ever imagined. Both sides of the abortion issue tugged at my emotions. I was stuck in the middle. I didn't know what to do. I felt bad for her, and I wanted to help her make the right decision, but I didn't know what that right decision was.

We talked some more, but nothing more was really said. When it was finally all said and done, I told her I would be there if she needed me, gave her a hug, and was on my way back home. The drive home was difficult, my headlights barely able to create a tunnel of light through the cold, misty fog of the dark, moonless night.

It didn't take long before I became lost in thought.

I sensed that the pressure of those around her would push her toward having an abortion. But she did have that look about her, and one's inner sense can be a powerful thing. Maybe someone who can help her through the pregnancy will step up and show her the way.

Then, a picture of that beautiful girl from biology class popped into my head. I was inspired. I wanted to be who that beautiful girl was, and say to my friend all she had said that day. I wanted to turn around, right then and there, turn around and tell her about all the great things that beautiful girl had said about the miracles of children and pregnancy. I wanted to somehow convince my friend that having the baby would be the right thing to do.

But there was a problem. I didn't know what to say, or how to say it. I wasn't listening to that beautiful girl that day in biology class; I never heard a word she said. I was too busy in my own thoughts, lost in a world of my own. I didn't care enough to pay even the slightest bit of attention.

I deflated.

My friend called me to help her make one of the most important decisions of her life. She had so many questions. I had none of the answers. The further I drove from her, the more I rationalized my ignorance. *This is getting too complicated. What will be, will be. You're looking into this too much. Let her decide for herself. Who am I to tell her what to do?*

I never turned around.

Yet the pain, the questions, and the anxiety in her face dogged my memory. That night, I watched as all of my friend's rational thought processes and internal inclinations give way to emotion, anxiety, and external pressures. Her life had become a blur, and she was dependent not on her own ability to make important decisions, but almost entirely on the advice and actions of others. Her all-important options were being shaped by the superficial opinions and beliefs offered by those around her who, like me, didn't know a thing about abortion or unborn human life. All she heard were voices telling her that having an abortion would be the best answer to her *problem* of being pregnant.

I sensed that in the end, this wasn't going to be her choice. It wasn't going to be her decision, for her own life. Someone was going to tell her what to do, tell her what they thought was right for her, tell her to have the abortion. And she would be able to do nothing else but listen to that voice.

She called me for help, but I couldn't help her. I didn't know anything about unborn human life or abortion. My attitudes and opinions toward abortion were formed on the fly, in an attempt to stay in the middle and avoid confrontation. I was helpless.

She came to me for answers.

My response was…the ultimate cop-out.

*****

A few weeks later, my friend called again, and I made another trip to see her. When I arrived, she told me that she had an abortion. She had been pregnant for eleven weeks.

We were eating lunch together when she looked up at me and said quietly, "I saw it."

I froze. "Saw what?"

"I saw the baby."

28

Saw the baby! Those words hit me like a brick. *There is no way,* I thought, *there is no way she could have seen anything, much less anything that looked like a real baby.*

I was at a loss for words. "You didn't."

"I did. It was about two inches long." She paused and looked down. "It was a boy."

My mind whirled. *Only eleven weeks! She was pregnant for only eleven weeks!* My mind raced to recall a picture from somewhere, anywhere, of an eleven-week-old baby in the womb. Nothing. *Two inches long. How could it have been that big?* I pictured in my head a tiny baby, two inches long, dead in a metal bedpan. *How could she have seen anything like this? Don't they knock the girls out? How would she ever get a look? It's not like the doctor is going to show her! Or maybe it fell on the floor?* I pictured this tiny baby on a dirty tile floor, surrounded in a pool of blood. A shiver shot up my spine. *Even if it did look like a little baby, there was no way she could tell it was a boy, not at eleven weeks.*

The rational side of my brain quickly stepped in and told me that it was just some miscellaneous tissue and blood, nothing in the form of a real baby. I shook my head. "You just think you…"

Her eyes beamed straight through me. "No, I saw the baby!" I could see in her eyes she was deeply hurt, disappointed that I didn't believe her. A tear began to slowly drip down her cheek.

I couldn't believe what she was telling me. The truth is, I didn't *want* to believe what she was telling me. I didn't want to believe there was a real baby involved with her abortion. I quickly made up my mind that this conversation was about events that were not real, and I was done. I had had enough. I was done with abortion. Done. I was done talking, done listening.

"You were pregnant for only eleven weeks. If it was anything, it was just a blob of tissue and blood. You saw nothing! You just think you saw something, you just imagined you saw something—I'm telling you, you saw nothing!"

She just stared back at me, blankly surprised at what I had just said.

For a quick moment, her eyes held mine. I couldn't help but look back, and deep within her eyes, I saw truth.

My friend was hurting deep inside. She wanted—no, needed—to tell me more about her baby, and her experience about the abortion procedure. But most of all, she needed me to believe her, believe what she said and somehow, share her pain. But I was done. This was more than I could deal with. I didn't want to believe her or share her pain.

I avoided her eyes and looked down.

The truth is, I knew right then and there that someway, somehow, she did see her tiny baby. Deep inside, I believed her. I knew she wasn't lying. She did see her tiny, two-inch baby boy—the baby boy that was taken care of during the abortion procedure.

But at the same time, I couldn't allow myself to fully accept this as reality. What she said didn't match the pictures of unborn human life, of abortion, I had painted for myself. She was trying to explain something to me that went against everything our pro-abortion society tells us about abortion—everything I was convinced to be true. *At worse, a girl's choice to have an abortion simply removed a glob of tissue and turned off her pregnancy. Abortion has nothing to do with a real baby. How could she have seen anything like a tiny baby? Isn't there a grace period of some sort?* What she told me didn't agree with these influences. What she was saying not only didn't make sense; it didn't seem possible.

Once again, I was caught in the middle of the abortion issue. This time, I had a decision to make. I could choose to accept my friend's firsthand experiences of abortion and unborn life as truth and reality, or I could choose to deny her experience on my own terms and consider everything she told me to be false, a fabrication of the mind.

I chose neither. I was uncomfortable with this conversation and I wanted out. After what seemed like an eternity, I finally looked up and then—

Changed the subject.

About Conceptualization

To Arrive at a Concept as a Result of Things Experienced or Believed

Even to this day, I think about my friend. I think about her and wonder if she ever goes back to that day in her life when she had the abortion. I wonder how different her life would have been if she didn't go to the clinic that day. I wonder if it would have been all that bad if she had her baby.

A few years later, my wife and I had our first child, a girl. Minutes after she was born, after the nurses bathed her with a sponge, and after the doctor examined her and administered all the required medications, I was holding her in my arms. There she was, brand new, only minutes old, all scrunched-up, pink, and beautiful. I couldn't help but think how precious my new baby girl was and, glancing across the room, how beautiful my wife looked in her post-birth glow and calm!

It was such a wonderful moment for this new dad. There in my arms was my new baby daughter, who just moments before was safely nestled within the womb of her mother. I realized right then and there, holding her all swaddled-up in a hospital blanket, a little pink cap on her head, that she was truly a miracle. I was in awe. I had just witnessed the greatest event ever to grace a man and a woman: the birth of their own baby.

That moment was life-changing.

I wish I could have stayed immersed in that moment forever, soaking into every inch of my being the love and beauty that surrounded me. But as it is, I'm just a guy, and it wasn't long before other guy thoughts began to seep into my mind. *How could this baby have been crammed in there?* I stared in disbelief at the belly of my wife. It didn't seem possible. *This baby is complete and all put together. How in the world did she ever fit?* I tried to imagine how my daughter could possibly have been all scrunched up inside my wife, flipped upside down, knees tucked up here, arms around here, head here, sucking her thumb. But nothing about this made any sense. *Her head, arms, legs, hands, feet…how in the world could all of this been all crammed within my wife's belly? How could there have been enough room?* Then probably the worst guy thought ever in the span of mankind hit me: *I can't believe she came out through there!*

Now, I had been present for my wife throughout the entire pregnancy. I didn't make it to all the doctor appointments, but I did show up for the important ones, the ones with the ultrasounds. Most of the time I didn't see exactly what the technician saw, but I knew that those swirling images were tracing the movements of a baby. I knew that the sound I heard was that of a beating heart.

I was a good husband and went with my wife to all the required natural childbirth classes. Here a labor and delivery nurse held up a baby doll and a pelvic bone, courtesy of a nearby skeleton, then in great detail demonstrated how the real baby would naturally position itself in the uterus, headfirst, then make its way down through the birth canal, squeezing its way out into its new world.

I was there to see the actual journey, the entire birthing process, start to finish. After what seemed like an eternity of labor, breathing, screaming, and pushing, the top of our baby's head finally emerged. Then, after a good amount of coaching from the nurse, my wife made another strong push and the rest of the head came through, our baby's face a deep shade of purple. After another push, her right shoulder and arm came flinging out. Then with a twist by the doctor, her left arm and shoulder flung out afterward. Then, with one more quick push and a little help from the doctor, her torso and legs emerged. Our baby was born into this world. "It's a girl!" I watched my daughter's face go from purple to pink as she drew in her first breaths of air. I heard her first cries. And even though I was a bit squeamish doing so, the doctor even let me cut the umbilical cord.

And there she was, our newborn baby girl.

Now, I know that everyone comes into this world for the most part the same way. Yet even after watching our baby grow within my wife for nine months, witnessing all the ultrasounds and having firsthand experience of the entire labor and birthing process, it all still seemed so impossible. I saw it, but it didn't make any sense. I was holding my daughter in my arms, yet it was difficult for me to come to terms with the reality that this baby, fully formed and all put together just as she was, was just minutes before neatly curled up inside the abdomen of my wife, patiently waiting for her cue to come out.

I'm not completely sure I expected anything else. It wasn't like I expected some gelatin-type ooze that was semi-formed in the shape of a baby to emerge from my wife, that when mixed with the air of the outside world ignited a miraculous reaction resulting in the for-mation of a real, live, baby. But still, the fact that this baby was, well, a real, fully formed baby inside the womb of my wife, seemed odd to me, and almost just as difficult to comprehend. Sure, I knew all of this growing and birthing stuff to be true, but I never fully realized it to be true. I couldn't fully see it in my mind to be true, and fully accept it in my mind to be true, until my daughter was born that day.

Only then did it all become truly real.

*****

A bit later, while still holding my baby daughter in the hospital delivery room, I recalled the memories of an old friend; a dark, rainy night; and a quiet lunch. I thought about my childhood friend, and what she had told me about her abortion. I heard again, her voice telling me that she had seen her tiny baby. *It was two inches long, a boy.* I flinched at the shock I felt, and at how I rationalized the denial of her experience. I knew that memory, I relived that memory, that memory was real. But that memory seemed to exist in a completely different world—a world of a long time ago, a cold world of confusion, darkness, and shadows. I looked around, and the realities of unborn life I had witnessed and experienced over the last nine months and in the delivery room that afternoon were as bright and clear as the light of day. But as my memories took me back in time, I saw only darkness and confusion.

I realized, right then and there under the bright lights of the hospital delivery room, that my newfound realities of a woman's unique ability to bear children, pregnancy, and existence of unborn life didn't come close to matching any of the self-conceived perceptions of potential life, globs of goo, and grace periods that I had created to justify being in the uncaring and non-confrontational center of the abortion issue. These newfound understandings were not even close to the pro-abortion viewpoint I was inundated with growing up.

I had a new picture of unborn human life and abortion: a perfectly clear picture that replaced the cloudy, abstract portrait I had painted for myself earlier in life. My new picture I *knew* to be real, and it was nothing like anything I had *believed* before. And this new picture, painted with the colors of new truths, was even more real because I learned them through the real events of pregnancy and childbirth.

As I stood there recalling the memory of my childhood friend, that dark cloud of the past transcended time and began to absorb the bright lights and sounds of the delivery room. A chill ran down my spine. *If my wife had chosen to have an abortion, that baby I saw in the ultrasounds would not have continued to grow, would not have been born on this day. If my wife had chosen to have an abortion, this beautiful baby, this tiny little girl that I was holding in my arms, would not...be.*

Yet I knew that when I saw my daughter and heard her in the ultrasounds, there was no doubt that while in the womb of her mother, she definitely...*was.*

I looked down at the face of my beautiful new daughter and gingerly brushed my fingers alongside her body. I saw truth. She was nothing else but alive within the protective womb of her mother from the moment she was conceived, she was and always had been *alive*. There could be no other way. She was alive from the very beginning, just as she was alive right now, here in my arms. But, if my wife had aborted her pregnancy, this baby, my daughter, all beautiful and pink, wouldn't be here. She wouldn't be alive anymore, she would have to be…dead.

As I moved deeper into these thoughts, the cold darkness of the past further engulfed my thoughts. I knew that my daughter was alive from the very beginning. I saw her, I heard her, alive in the ultrasounds. She was alive from the start. But after an abortion? No, she wouldn't be alive anymore. I thought again of my friend and sickness filled my stomach. She would have been…killed.

*****

Killed. That's what I knew that day. I knew that unborn life is real from conception—a human baby is alive from the moment of conception. When a woman aborts her baby, the baby *must be* killed. That is what I knew after realizing firsthand the realities of pregnancy and childbirth. My new pictures of unborn life and abortion were as clear as the light of day.

But it didn't take long for these pictures to cloud back up again, and become as blurry and vague as they were back in my high school days.

Today's conversation of life is dominated by pro-abortion voices dictating a virtuous message of abortion for women and society. Like what that girl in my biology class experienced, attempting to relate anything to the contrary quickly becomes a lesson in futility. I tried to tell others what I realized to be true about unborn human life, using my experiences and personal beliefs in an attempt to back me up. But anytime I started up on my pro-life spiel, I was quickly silenced, belittled, and accused of being judgmental. I was enlightened by pro-abortion voices that my experiences were…just *my experiences* and nothing more, that what I came to know that day in the hospital delivery room was only a confirmation of *my personal feelings* and *subjective thoughts* toward unborn life. Revelations that I knew had to be objectively true were recognized as nothing but perceptions that I only *thought* were true. They were just some of the many different and varying *subjective perceptions* used to define unborn human life within today's conversation of life.

And my thoughts, feelings, and beliefs were on the wrong side of the conversation.

The sharp, detailed colors that represented the beauty of unborn life and the horrors of abortion in my pictures once again blurred together, no longer clearly representing what I had previously known—or was it only what I had *thought* I had known?—as truth.

I had settled into thinking that maybe they were right and I was wrong. The sheer intensity in which the pro-abortion message is promoted in today's society, and the fierceness in which the belief that an unborn human baby is alive from conception is attacked, put down, and censored, led to a gnawing sense of uncertainty within me. Maybe there was something more to the abortion issue than what I thought I knew; something that nullified what I believed. *There must be a good reason why abortion can be legal in America. There must be something more to abortion that I don't know, something that in a way I didn't know, somehow makes it right, makes it okay.*

I still didn't think abortion was right, but maybe…it wasn't as wrong as I thought.

Soon enough, my portrait of unborn human life and picture of abortion once again became nothing more than the superficial depictions of what the influences found in today's conversation of life wanted me to see: colors shallow in knowledge, fact and truth, but deep in ignorance, convenience, cowardice, confusion, and conformity toward the issues of unborn human life and abortion.

I was pushed back into the middle of the issue.

Like my childhood friend, my picture of unborn human life, my feelings and emotions toward abortion, were being pulled from two different directions—one from the inside, the other from the outside.

*****

Let's go back to the original question from the beginning of this book. Which picture do you see when you think of abortion? Are you somewhere in the middle, like I was during my high-school days; there because you just don't know any better; and you don't want to make any waves? Maybe you accept that unborn life exists, painted through a religious belief or personal revelation. Or maybe you see a political battle over women's rights; that you don't believe government should have the right to tell you what to do with your body. Or maybe you want to be a pro-life voice, but have been bullied back into the middle.

Wherever you stand, ask yourself, how did I get here? How has today's conversation of life influenced you into determining the pictures of unborn human life and abortion you have painted for yourself? Have you simply latched onto a political position? A religious belief? A societal justification? A personal moral code? Have you painted your pictures of unborn human life and abortion, and call them truth, based on your position toward these issues? Or are your pictures of unborn human life and abortion based on truth, and through truth you have based your position toward abortion?

Let's take a closer look into today's conversation of life, and the pictures of unborn human life and abortion it paints for society. Let's see if we can find any truth within today's abortion debate, and which side of the debate the truth resides.

About Observations

Remarks Based on Something Seen, Heard, or Noticed

What about today's conversation of life? How is this conversation played out in society today? When we actually take time to pay attention to what is being said, and to who is saying it, we find some very interesting observations…and contradictions.

*****

Since the Supreme Court's 1973 ruling in Roe v. Wade, any woman choosing to end her unwanted pregnancy with an abortion is hailed throughout the mainstream media as a woman with complete control and authority over her body, her womanhood, and her reproductive capability—a true hero for the cause of women's rights.

But there is another side to this heroic feminism. What if the husband of this same woman finds out, *before* she's able to have the abortion, that she is carrying the baby of another man? What if in a fit of rage, he brutally attacks this woman and strangles her, killing her while she's still pregnant with the unborn baby? This tragic event would be reported as the brutal killing of a woman *and* her unborn child, a tragedy of domestic violence against a mother *and* her baby. Headlines and voices throughout the mainstream media would justly proclaim, "The husband has been apprehended and is now in police custody. He is expected to be charged with the double murder of his pregnant wife and her unborn baby."

Here we have two completely different public perceptions toward what is essentially the same end for the unborn baby.

In the first case, the unborn baby is not considered to be, in any sense of the matter, alive, and is therefore *only aborted* by its mother: the irrelevant consequence of a mother's decision to end her pregnancy. In the second case, the unborn baby is considered fully alive in every sense of the matter, and therefore is *brutally killed:* the relevant consequence of an evil decision made by a killer.

These are two very different scenarios involving the same fate for the same unborn baby. How is it that American society can consider the death of an unborn baby in one scenario to be due to the actions of a violent killer being charged as a criminal, and in the other the same fate recognized and promoted as nothing more than the inconsequential result of a legal choice made by…a hero?

*****

In any United States court, if there is not enough hard evidence to convict a defendant, that is, if there is any reasonable doubt present regarding the guilt of the defendant, then that defendant must be declared not guilty.

If it is true that there is no consensus on when human life begins, or on which of the many different and contradictory personal perceptions of unborn life truly defines the existence of human life within the womb, isn't there then a reasonable doubt to the legitimacy of any of the claims? If someone claims that "There probably isn't life" within the womb, then that statement could also be interpreted as "There could be life" within the womb. If the current abortion laws are based on "There probably isn't life" within the womb, then it's entirely possible that the current abortion laws are legalizing the killing of babies that "could be alive" within the womb.

Likewise, if the main debate within the abortion issue is whether the unborn baby is alive, or not alive, wouldn't you think that the

1973 United States Supreme Court would have erred on the side of alive, applying the precedent of reasonable doubt for the sake of protecting the life, even if it was only a *potential* life, of the unborn baby?

But they didn't.

*****

Certain statements made within the abortion debate make perfect sense when applied specifically to the abortion issue, but become outright foolish when applied outside the issue. Take, for instance, this story that I heard about a pro-abortion politician who was in a hurry to wrap up a press meeting. Finishing up, she was asked this unexpected question, "When does the life of a baby begin?"

Not prepared for such a question, she quickly responded, "When the mother says so."

When the mother says so?

This slip of the tongue clearly shows a discomforting perspective on the choice a woman makes on abortion. While it is true that women are allowed the choice of abortion, this choice cannot be the determining factor on whether the baby within her womb is alive or not alive.

*****

Statements such as "When the mother says so" usually don't make it into mainstream media news reports. Instead, the media is more likely to report on abortion conversations that relate more to what we normally hear in an abortion discussion, and are more consistent with what we seemingly want to hear.

Nowhere has both sides of the conversation of life been so concisely presented to the American public than during the 2008 presidential debate at Saddleback Church, between Barack Obama and John McCain. During this debate, both candidates were asked a simple question meant to publicly define for the nation each candidate's personal philosophy and their political party's position regarding abortion.

The question: "Forty million abortions, at what point does a baby get human rights, in your view?"

To fully recognize the meaning and the point behind this question, we must understand that any baby that is considered to be *human,* and *alive,* would be considered a "person" within the law and therefore protected under the provisions of the Constitution. This "person" would be afforded all *human rights* allowed within federal law. This, of course, includes the right to life within the womb.

In other words, the real question that was asked in this presidential debate was the same question that is argued and debated in abortion-related discussions across America: "In your view, when do you believe human life begins?"

The Democrat candidate, Barack Obama, was first to speak. He stepped up and stated that, "Answering that question with specificity, you know, is above my pay grade." Mr. Obama went on to state that abortion was an issue that "obviously the country wrestles with," admitting that there is "a moral and ethical element to this issue" and anyone attempting to deny these "difficulties" is "not paying attention." Then he went on to say that he is "pro-choice," and that he believed in Roe v. Wade because he didn't think women make these decisions casually, that "They wrestle with these things in profound ways."

Here Mr. Obama is simply pleading a blameless ignorance toward the origination of unborn human life, as well as the subtle implication that it is pointless in attempting to search out a real answer. He then goes on to inform the American public that women have some sort of unique ability to "wrestle" with this question on their own, and somehow through this innate sense create their own moral justification regarding the issue.

He never directly answers the question. Instead, he simply redirects to a woman's right to choose. This is the pro-abortion platform.

The blameless ignorance of the pro-abortion argument is based on the widely promoted belief that there is no agreement on the exact moment in time when an unborn baby becomes "alive." Therefore, pro-abortion voices illustrate that the actual reality of unborn life is up for individual interpretation. And as Mr. Obama states, since women "Wrestle with these things in profound ways," women are well enough qualified, based solely on their gender, to figure out on their own whether or not their unborn baby is alive. Truly, *when the mother says so.*

Pro-abortion voices always redirect questions regarding the existence of unborn life to the current constitutional right of allowing women to decide for themselves when the presence of unborn life exists, or whether life even matters. This way, the abortion issue does indeed boil down to an issue of choices: a woman's choice to believe as she wishes, choose as she wishes, and justify her decisions as she wishes.

Next up to answer the question was the Republican presidential candidate, Senator John McCain. Senator McCain spoke up, answering the question with undoubted confidence, "At the moment of conception." His concise reply apparently said it all, much to the applause of the largely pro-life audience.

Senator McCain's statement that human life begins from the moment of conception is a primary pro-life argument, and as is usual in this discussion, nothing else was said. Senator McCain didn't offer any additional explanation or insight behind why he believed, or possibly learned or knew, that human life begins at conception. He didn't provide any additional proof—proof of life that might have been more convincing or non-faith related, to factually back up and better defend his statement.

In not further confirming his answer, Senator McCain implied to the pro-abortion mainstream media that he was expecting the American public, regardless of social or theological conviction, to accept as undeniable truth, his personal belief that unborn life begins at the moment of conception. Take it or leave it.

The media left it.

So, there it was, presented in its entirety for all of America to hear, consider, and decide upon; the abortion conversation, the conversation of life in America. This made-for-media performance was perfectly consistent with the same abortion debate that we've all grown accustomed to through the mainstream media. The question sounded presidential, but it was the same. The well-rehearsed replies of the candidates, perfect, exactly what each side wanted to hear.

*****

In 2009 Sonia Sotomayor was appointed to the United States Supreme Court. To fulfill America's desire for an official statement regarding her position on abortion, we were informed by the mainstream media that she believed, "Roe v. Wade is a matter of settled law."

The media didn't report much else regarding this position on abortion, which leaves a lot to implication. Surely, her response indicates a pro-abortion position, in that the abortion issue in America has been legally settled in the highest court of the land, and therefore supposedly not up for discussion. Her response implies too, that she must also tow the same pro-abortion line when it comes to other related discussions: "Abortion is nothing more than a woman's choice, a woman's choice to decide for herself the life and humanity of the baby she is carrying," "That the abortion procedure doesn't actually kill the unborn baby, that the baby isn't alive until it is fully born from its mother." It could also be assumed that her response was to a question that was the same as, or similar to, the one asked a year earlier in the presidential debate: "Forty million abortions, at what point does a baby get human rights?"

But that isn't true. In this case, Justice Sotomayor was simply asked by a pro-abortion senator, "In your opinion, is *Roe* settled law?" This is an extremely soft question for a potential Supreme Court justice during a senate confirmation hearing, especially on a topic as controversial and emotional as abortion. Yet it was asked, and her answer fit the bill, and the press loved it. Interestingly enough, later in the hearings, when a pro-life senator attempted to coax Justice Sotomayor into further explaining her position on abortion, she offered no additional details, except that *Roe* was "a matter of settled law."

Why was Justice Sotomayor fed such a softball question during a Supreme Court confirmation hearing by her pro-abortion government counterpart? And furthermore, why did she completely avoid additional details regarding her pro-abortion stand when further questioned by a pro-life senator? Why didn't she just state, "The baby isn't really alive; it just depends on what the pregnant woman thinks. It really isn't a baby anyway"? No, instead she never went outside the safety of "Roe v. Wade is a matter of settled law."

Was she trying to hide something?

Could it be, that the unspoken reason why Justice Sotomayor didn't state the standard pro-abortion platform—"The baby isn't alive, the baby isn't killed. Abortion is simply a choice and nothing more"—is that she couldn't? Could it be that she couldn't express these viewpoints and at the same time present them as truth? Could it be that she avoided stating the standard pro-abortion arguments regarding the life, or non-life, of the unborn baby because she knows and understands that they aren't true? Not in science, not in medicine, not even in United States law?

About Science

Knowledge, as Distinguished from Ignorance or Misunderstanding

B y now, one question has to be burning in your mind: *Is there an answer to when human life begins?*

Today, pro-life voices are constantly under attack for being on the wrong side of the abortion conversation. Pro-abortion advocates adamantly dismiss any pro-life claims that unborn human life exists from the moment of conception, declaring these thoughts to be nothing more than one's wayward individual philosophy or religious fabrication of thought. "Keep your religion off my body." "Science is real, your beliefs aren't." Pro-life voices imply that science is on their side, that science is unclear on when human life begins, and therefore any foolish pro-life stand to the contrary against abortion must be based on nothing but philosophical, or theological, crock.

We are inundated by the popular media with unquestionable surety that there is no full consensus, anywhere, as to when, or if, an unborn baby ever becomes alive, and that the recognition of unborn human life can only be up to an individual's—especially a pregnant woman's—beliefs, feelings, and convictions to decide. It is implied too, that the question of unborn human life is so difficult to assess, it is fruitless even attempting to find an answer. This is the dominant pro-abortion message broadcast throughout society. Decade after decade of this debate has brought us no closer to a concrete resolution to this question of when unborn human life begins.

But if you stop and think about this for a moment, something about this pro-abortion argument doesn't make sense. How could there truly be no agreement within the world of science, and the interlocking field of medicine, as to when human life originates? If this is truly the case, then doesn't it seem odd—especially for the medical life sciences that specifically study human life itself—that there is no consensus on the precise moment in time when the human life that they are studying *actually* begins? Thinking on this point a bit deeper, isn't it odd that medical scientists can generate and grow living entities inside a laboratory dish, but cannot know the parameters necessary to define those entities as *living* in the first place?

And on the other side of the spectrum, if medicine or science cannot determine precisely when human life begins, how then, can they precisely define when it ends?

Then what about the *legal* aspects of life and death? Within every aspect of our laws, science in its relation to medicine, and medicine in its relation to science, especially when human life and death is involved, must be completely understood, specified, and fully defined. This careful attention to the relationship between law, science, and medicine must exist to assure that every legal, moral, and ethical challenge to the law can not only be determined, but be well understood, specified, and wholly defined. Wouldn't you think that our own legal system would demand that a precise time in which the unborn baby possesses life be positively determined and agreed upon within science and medicine?

*****

Truth is, finding the answer to when human life begins is easy. You only have to know where to look. Science possesses the answer. The problem with today's conversation of life is that it revolves in the *wrong type* of science.

Today's conversation of life revolves around a litany of many and varying individual attitudes, personal feelings, and beliefs regarding the existence of unborn human life. We relate to unborn human life based primarily on what we believe, or feel, to be true. "I believe the baby is alive from conception." "Keep your beliefs off my body." "My body, my decision." These attitudes and perceptions, on both sides of the issue, are formed largely in and around one's own personal *philosophy*, which may or may not include one's theology, toward abortion and human life.

The problem with basing a conversation regarding the existence of human life on one's philosophy is that philosophy is a *social science*, not a *physical science*. In a physical science, questions such as unborn human life are answered through observed phenomena and natural law. The social science of philosophy, however, doesn't definitively define anything. Instead, it is simply a process of thought: one where individuals discern and internally decide for themselves the meaning of a question, thereby allowing them to arrive at their own *subjective conclusion* based on nothing more than their own personal feelings, perceptions, beliefs, convictions, and prejudices. Because answers to philosophical questions are subjective, or true to the beholder, there will never be one definite answer. Instead, the answers can be as numerous as the number of individuals giving them. And since each answer is simply a reflection of what one believes, or feels, to be true, each one must be considered as such.

In other words, philosophy allows one to decide for himself what is real and true. Everyone is right.

Can you see the problem here? We argue the ultimate question of whether a human baby is alive within the womb based on what? Subjective feelings and individual perceptions! The ultimate question in today's conversation of life *demands* a definitive answer. Yet today's abortion conversation continuously revolves in and around personal beliefs and convictions, in and around the social science of philosophy; and philosophy doesn't definitively define anything.

It's no wonder there is complete disagreement in today's abortion debate as to the beginning of human life. From the age of Socrates to the present, societies have attempted to explain their human existence based on perceptions, feelings and beliefs—each reaching their own conclusions in light of their societal education, living environments, and social-cultural values. Through the social science of philosophy, we are open to a cornucopia of beliefs and feelings attempting to define the existence or non-existence of unborn human life, because everyone is open to developing their own perspectives and opinions based not necessarily on objective fact and observation, but solely upon what *life* means to them.

One's individual perspective toward human life is never used to dictate the actual existence of life in any medical setting or court of law. Philosophy *cannot and does not* define the exact parameters of human life and death. How then can the social science of philosophy be used to debate an issue that involves whether an unborn human baby is alive or not alive?

The answer is...*it can't.*

*****

The existence of unborn human life, and when it begins, is not something that can be personally considered, contemplated, and then drawn to an individual conclusion. The *knowledge* of unborn human life, and the precise moment at which it begins, is something that *must be learned.*

The very existence of human life and the precise moment in which this life begins is absolutely defined within the universally accepted laws of *physical science.*

Within the laws of physical science (a law being a universally accepted *objective* truth, true forever and always) human beings are classified as *organisms.* Being scientifically classified as organisms, humans possess a very specific trait common among all organisms. All organisms are *defined* as an organism through the *existence* of life. Life must absolutely exist for an organism to be defined and classified as an organism. All organisms are capable of life. All organisms are alive. This is unless, of course, the organism in question is dead. Yet this is another specific trait common among all organisms: any living organism will eventually become a dead organism.

But for death to come to an organism, it must have first become alive.

Not everything on this earth has the capability to become alive, to possess life, and therefore die. For all other things that are not classified as organisms, or capable of life, there is only one other major scientific category. This other category is called *inorganic matter*. Inorganic matter includes *things* and *objects:* cars, rocks, clothing, shampoo, computers, traffic signs, tables, books, etc. None of these things can ever become alive; none of these objects can ever become an organism.

We find here some very important facts that we must pull out if we are going to determine through scientific knowledge and truth when an unborn baby becomes alive.

First: Absolutely everything on this planet is scientifically classified as either an organism, whether alive or dead, or inorganic matter, not capable of life. Everything that exists on earth today can only be placed into one of these two categories. There is no classification for almost inorganic matter, or not-quite-yet an organism.

Second: There are only two states of existence possible for an organism: alive or dead. An organism can only be in one of these states of existence at any given time. It is important to fully understand that an organism is defined as an organism by the sheer fact of becoming alive. There is no almost-alive period or not-quite-yet-alive state of being. There is no period of time when an organism waits in some sort of a limbo until it reaches a certain stage of development when it can at last, finally become, an actual living organism.

Thirdly: Inorganic matter can never turn into, or evolve into, an organism; just as an organism, be it dead or alive, can never become inorganic matter. There is no natural ability for anything to transfer from one distinction to another.

The shadows and darkness that surround the question of unborn human life are now beginning to clear. If science clearly distinguishes between what can be alive and what can't be alive, then science must have a very distinct and precise protocol for determining not only the capability of but the very presence of *life*.

*****

You are a living organism. What are you doing right now that makes you capable of life? What is going on within you that makes you, alive? You are breathing, check. Your heart is beating, check. Your brain is initiating electrical impulses that travel throughout your body, check. There are others to be sure, but these are the three main functions most come up with. The truth is, these are just a few of the thousands of functions going on within your body that all work together to make you capable of life.

But do these specific functions define the *existence* of life within you?

Life must exist at some point in time within all organisms. And of course, for any organism to sustain life, however long or brief it may be, certain operations or functions must occur.

But to be alive—that is, in order to live—different organisms function in very different and distinct ways. For instance, we humans sustain life in a manner that is considerably different from those of fish, yet both humans and fish are living organisms. Fish maintain life through functions that are much different than those of a tree, and yet fish and trees are living organisms. And even still, the functions a tree must process to maintain life are much different from those of bacteria, yet trees and bacteria are both also scientifically classified organisms.

When defining the existence of life, we must take into consideration *all* forms of life. When taking into consideration the entire classification of living organisms, a beating heart, breathing through lungs, and brain function *cannot* be the criteria used to define the existence of life, simply because not all organisms utilize these specific functions to live. This is clearly evident as jellyfish don't have heartbeats, trees don't breathe through lungs, and bacteria don't survive on their ability to reason.

Yet these three functions—lung function, heartbeats, and brain activity—are used by many in an attempt to define the existence of life, or lack of life, within the human organism, especially human life within the womb.

This is wrong.

In reality, any organism, including a human organism, must do certain things that are much more specific than have a beating heart, functioning lungs, or an active brain to be considered alive. For any organism to be defined as alive, it must be doing some very particular things. First: *Growing.* Second: *Reacting to the environment.* Third: *Reproducing, both cellular and individual.* When considering the entire classification of organisms, this doesn't necessarily involve heartbeats, breathing through lungs, or electrical nerve function.

There is one more thing, one more process that must presently occur if an organism is to be defined as *alive.* This function is the single most important one of any organism, for this function involves the energy necessary for life itself. Fact is, all life requires energy. Without energy, life could not exist. The universal laws of energy— the physical laws of thermodynamics—define this intimate relationship between energy and life.

Quite simply, to be defined as alive, all living organisms must somehow access energy from their surroundings, and *metabolize* it, in some way, shape, or form, so to sustain life. More precisely, living organisms must access energy from their surroundings and metabolize it, so that the functions of growing, reacting, and reproducing can occur.

Metabolism has two primary functions within any living organism. First, organisms take in types of energy that it may not be able to readily use, and metabolize them into other types of energy that it can readily use in order to function and live. Secondly, an organism will take in different types of energy, and break them down to metabolize them into new substances that will allow them to grow, react, and reproduce.

For life to exist within an organism, there must be energy. For life to exist, organisms must actively take in available energy from outside sources and metabolize it to provide the usable energy and chemical resources necessary for life.

Metabolism of energy is the key to life. When you find metabolism, you find life.

*****

At the very moment the male sperm enters the female egg, the energy stored within these two entities is released, metabolized, and partially consumed in the formation of the very first cell of a brand-new human being. Once formed, this cell draws from a reserve of chemical energy to divide, divide, and divide again, until it becomes a group of cells. Soon, this group of cells attaches itself to the inside of the woman's uterus, where it consumes and metabolizes the energy available in this blood supply until the placenta and umbilical cord are formed. The baby then consumes and metabolizes the nutrients within this blood supply the same way that all humans do, utilizing the energy and chemical components to grow, react to the environment, and continue with cellular reproduction.

The metabolism of energy begins at the precise moment the male sperm enters the female egg: at the very moment of conception.

Human life begins at the moment of conception.

*****

Well now, that was easy.

Maybe, though, that was just a bit too easy.

The simple fact that these parameters of life are so well defined, and so easy to find, creates an air of uncertainty when applying these scientific laws to the existence of life within humans, especially unborn humans. According to the prevailing notion of today's pro-abortion media outlets, there is no definitive point in time when an unborn baby becomes alive. If we have based our perceptions toward unborn life on this well-promoted notion, then we too must believe that somewhere there must be a variation within these laws that alters this scientific reality when applied to an unborn human baby. After all, we humans aren't just any kind of organism. We are, well, human; above all other creatures. Given the intensity of the ongoing public debate on unborn human life, something *must* be different in defining the existence of life within humans. The answer to the origination of human life can't possibly be so straightforward.

Or could it?

To further answer this question of precisely when human life is initiated, we once again look into science. Only this time we consider a more specific science: a life science. The science of *embryology* is a medical life science that specifically studies the early stages of human conception, growth, and formation. Here we find that the medical life science of embryology defines the origination of human life in very specific and well-defined terms:

> Fertilization is a sequence of events...that begins with the contact of a sperm (spermatozoon) with a secondary oocyte (ovum) and ends with the fusion of their pronuclei (the haploid nuclei of the sperm and ovum) and the mingling of their chromosomes to form a new cell...This fertilized ovum, known as a zygote...is a large diploid cell that is the beginning, or primordium, of a human being. Human development [requiring energy] begins after the union of male and female gametes or germ cells during a process known as fertilization [conception].[1]

The medical life science of embryology absolutely defines, and precisely determines, the exact point in time at which the life of a human begins: *at the precise moment of conception.*

It is now clear. Contrary to what we are constantly inundated with through the pro-abortion media, there aren't two or more contradictory versions of truth regarding the beginning of human life. There cannot be two or more contradictory versions of when or if an unborn baby becomes alive. There is only one truth, one reality to the origination of human life.

The real truth is, human life begins precisely at the very moment of conception.

---

[1]   Keith L. Moore, Essentials of Human Embryology (Toronto, B.C. Decker Inc, 1988), 2.

This is the real conversation of life.

*****

This is the true picture of unborn human life and when it begins, as defined in medicine and science. Yet this revelation goes completely against everything we are exposed to through the popular mainstream media. Within this precise definition, we find that the beginning of human life is not up for individual interpretation. We find that there *is* an exact point in time at which human life begins, and this moment is clearly specified and defined in the laws—universally recognized as truth forever and always—of physical science and medicine.

This objective truth defining the origin of human life is accessible, easy to understand, and absolutely clear. There is nothing within this objective reality of life that is above anybody's "pay grade."

*****

Now that we know when human life begins, when does human life end? This is quite simple. The natural life cycle of any organism, including all humans, will end when metabolism ceases. When a human is no longer metabolizing the energy necessary to sustain life, the human is no longer alive. The human is now dead.

Once an organism is dead, when a human organism is dead, the only natural process left to occur is—decay.

About Origin

The Point at Which Something
Comes into Existence

W e have now found that the unborn human baby is alive from the moment of conception. This may come as a shock to some, and for them there may still be some doubt. For others it may be the welcome confirmation of what they previously thought or believed to be true. Either way, it's difficult to come to terms with the reality that this is an objective scientific and medical truth, only because for decades we have been inundated to believe that there is no exact point in time when an unborn baby is confirmed to be alive, that an unborn baby is only alive when the mother says so.

Yet we find it clearly documented and recognized that the human baby is alive at conception.

Over the last five decades, we have been led to believe that having an abortion has nothing to do with the actual killing of an unborn baby. We have been indoctrinated that an abortion is nothing more than a decision, a choice made by a pregnant woman to end her pregnancy; a decision to not be pregnant anymore. Yet, we have found that it is scientifically and medically clear that an unborn baby is truly and fully alive within the womb from conception. This is an objective truth. For a woman to become un-pregnant through an abortion procedure, then the living human baby within her womb *must* be killed.

How has this knowledge of life been hidden from us?

History shows that one of the most effective ways to hide the existence of human life in a conversation is to hide humanity.

When you pay attention, you find that today's pro-abortion popular media doesn't refer to an unborn human baby with warmth and affection as an *unborn baby* or an *unborn child*. Instead, we hear the media refer to a human baby within the womb of its mother rather coldly and without feeling, using medical terms such as a *zygote*, an *embryo*, or *fetus;* or descriptive phrases like "a sack of tissue," "an appendage," or just "a glob of tissue and blood, just part of a woman's body." When the media presents us with these impressive words, we don't picture in our minds an image of a developing unborn baby. Instead, we picture something that is not yet a baby, not yet human, and not yet fully alive. We see in our mind's eye something that might very well almost be, but is still not quite, a real living baby. This promotion of a non-human, non-living glob of nothing but miscellaneous tissue and blood is fully demonstrated when we hear pro-abortion medical and legal voices attempt to redefine and reclassify an aborted human baby as nothing but "a byproduct of conception."

A human baby, redefined and reclassified as only a byproduct of conception, considered nothing more than medical waste.

*****

Back in 2008, two presidential hopefuls were asked a simple question meant to outline their personal and political position on abortion: At what point does a baby get human rights? This question is at the heart of today's conversation of life because one's answer reflects their acceptance or denial of the two factors necessary for any "person" to attain the protections outlined within the United States Constitution. These two factors are life and humanity. In other words, one's answer to this question is the simple affirmation of when one recognizes when the unborn baby is fully alive, and when it is fully human.

The perception promoted through today's powerful pro-abortion media is that the unborn child is not only possibly not alive but not necessarily even human. This perception has effectively *dehumanized* the unborn child. In the mind's eye of the American public, the unborn baby is painted as nothing but a formless glob of tissue and blood, and should the woman say so, just an inconvenient medical condition, a disposable threat to her freedom and enemy to her lifestyle—one that can easily be taken care of.

Dehumanizing human life is nothing new. History has shown time and again how dehumanization has been used by those in power to deal with, or do away with, those determined to be unwanted, undesirable, or simply unworthy of life. The ultimate destruction of defiled and unwanted persons becomes even more justifiable when they are painted as an enemy to society or a threat to one's way of life—something that is better off, or makes you better off, when they are dead.

Extremes of dehumanization occurred during the 1930s and 40s, when Adolf Hitler and his Nazi leadership determined that the Jewish people were primarily to blame for the problems of the world and a viable threat to the purity of the German master race and their quest for world domination. Josef Goebbels, the "Minister of Public Enlightenment and Propaganda" for the Nazi party, devised a plan called the Final Solution to deal with this Jewish problem. His plan called for the total annihilation of Jews not only in Germany, but around the world. The Final Solution was quickly expanded to include the old, the sick, homosexuals, those of other unwanted nationalities, and others considered problematic to society and detrimental to the true majesty of German life.

It is important to understand at this point, especially in relationship to the abortion issue in America, that the indoctrination of the public hatred toward Jews and other unwanted peoples that was necessary for the successful implementation and continuation of the deadly actions of the Final Solution, originated through the creation and advancement of *specific legislation* that *legally dehumanized and redefined* the humanity of Jews and other targeted peoples within German law.

In other words, Jews and other unwanted peoples within German society had to first be redefined, reclassified, and dehumanized within German law. The legal creation of a lower-than-human perception of Jews and other targeted peoples made it easy for the German public to accept and act upon as their human right, the complete destruction and annihilation of Jews and those deemed a threat to their lifestyle.

Once Jews and other unwanted peoples were dehumanized within the law, and their ultimate destruction made a legal right of any true German citizen, the Nazi leadership turned to a massive "public enlightenment" campaign meant to filter unrest and hatred toward these people down throughout all of German society. This campaign maximized the power and influence of all forms of available popular media to form and promote the necessary public perceptions and attitudes that made the oppression and slaughter of these unwanted and unworthy, not-quite-human forms of life more than just acceptable, but a civic duty, the legal right of any real German citizen.

From there, the Nazi government simply left it up to the individual German citizen, those who believed in the necessity and prosperity promised in this propaganda, to take over and work their part for the betterment of their lives and German society. The agenda of this propaganda campaign was a huge success. From the eyes of the Nazi leaders all the way down through the entire German population, Jews and other undesirables became viewed as nothing more than trash, rats, vermin, parasites, the lowest of low, scum: an undesirable, less-than-human species that stood in the way of the great German master race; undesirable creatures declared expendable, not worthy of life.

The result of the mass public hysteria in the Holocaust is well-known. Millions of Jewish men, women, and children, as well as other undesirable races and the sick and needy, were stripped of their humanity, their citizenship, and their rights, forcibly removed from their homes to be rounded up, oppressed, tortured, and killed, all at the will of any real German citizen, any true German "hero."

Nazi leaders justified the agenda, implementation, and public promotion of the Final Solution in the name of subjective social reasoning, societal economic illusions, and perceived lifestyle improvement.

*****

America has not been immune from similar attacks on humanity—attacks formally instituted through our own legal system. In one of the most infamous decisions in United States Supreme Court history, the 1857 Supreme Court decided that slavery was a constitutional right in America, and any attempts to restrict or prohibit slavery in America were unconstitutional. The justification for this mass injustice toward humanity was done by declaring within the court's ruling that "slaves and children of slaves, those 'negroes of African descent,' were not considered to be fully human within the interpretation of United States federal law." As specifically stated within the ruling of the landmark Dred Scott v. Sanford case, these "negroes" were determined within the parameters of United States law to be nothing more than…

> beings of an inferior order; and altogether unfit to associate with the white race…either in social or political relations…and so far inferior that they had no rights which the white man was bound to respect…neither negroes of African descent nor their descendants were embraced in any of the other provisions of the Constitution.

With the stroke of a pen by the United States Supreme Court, any person of "this unfortunate race" in America was officially *dehumanized* and *reclassified* within the law, reduced to a lower species of being, legally downgraded to a species considered within the law as not-quite-fully-human. In this Supreme Court decision, people "of African descent" were legally declared to be nothing other than another man's property, an animal, a species unequal to white humans, and therefore unworthy of any human rights granted within the American Constitution. African Americans within the United

States, like the Jewish people in Nazi Germany, were stripped of their humanity, their citizenship, and their basic human rights, rounded up, oppressed, forced into inhumane working and living conditions, used as farm beasts, tortured, raped, and killed—their very lives subject to the will and whim of the real southern American citizen—any true Southern "hero."

The justification of slavery in America also came in the name of subjective social reasoning, societal economic illusions, and perceived lifestyle improvement.

*****

Today, another segment of society has been dehumanized. Through the American legal system, via the public interpretation of the Roe v. Wade ruling, the unborn human baby has been redefined, reclassified, and accepted within the law as a lower-level being, a second-class being not worthy of any human rights. This dehumanization has promoted the perception within the mind's eye of the American public that the unborn baby is not quite a real human baby—that it is nothing more than a formless glob of tissue, just part of a woman's body, hers to deal with as she pleases. As a result, over 50 million unborn human babies have been deemed undesirable, unnecessary mental burdens, financial drains, detriments to society, threats to one's independence, or simply unwanted, and therefore, unworthy of life. Unborn human children have been denied their humanity, their citizenship, and their basic human rights, convicted of standing in the way of women's progress, and then simply taken care of. The very life of an unborn baby has become dependent upon whether "a mother says so," a true feminist "hero."

As seen before in other historical times of tragic social injustice, this dehumanization occurs in the name of perceived lifestyle improvement, societal economic illusions, and subjective social reasoning.

*****

Vladimir Lenin, the first leader of the Soviet Union, was the first to officially declare this new war on this new enemy. In 1920, after rising to power following the bloody Russian revolution, and after instituting the Great Purge in which he authorized the slaughter of the prior ruling class and anyone deemed to be a threat to his regime, Lenin, in one of his first acts in office, legalized the institution of abortion in Russia. This made Russia the first nation in the world to do so.

Was Vladimir Lenin an activist for the feminist cause? Was he so mindful and in tune with the social/medical welfare of women plagued with unplanned and unwanted pregnancies that in coming to power he wanted to assure that Russia would be the first in the world to legalize abortion through a woman's right to privacy?

I am going to bet no. I am going to say he had other motives, but this is a discussion for another day.

*****

So then, what does it mean to be *human?* Does being human involve the capacity to think, to learn, and to conceive rational solutions to problems? Is it that we can walk on two feet, or swing a baseball bat? Does our humanity depend upon the development of two lungs, one heart, two arms, etc.? If these are the criteria that define our humanity, then what about those who have a lesser mental capacity? Those who can't walk or swing a baseball bat, or those born with only one lung, a defective heart, or half an arm? What about a baby that is still developing these human characteristics? Does this make the unborn baby not-quite-human, a lower species of being?

When we consider the ways in which abortion is justified, it is necessary to understand that being human has little to do with our capacity to think, the finished product of our bodies, or one's ability to do certain activities. Being human depends solely upon meeting one criteria: *human DNA.* Human DNA defines the human being.

Upon conception, when the male sperm enters the female egg, twenty-three chromosomes from the female egg and twenty-three chromosomes from the male sperm combine to form the chromosomes that make up the DNA of a brand new, independent human being. Conceived with a complete blueprint for development, this first cell, and all subsequent cells, will metabolize the necessary energy to grow, react, and reproduce, eventually forming and maintaining the organism we call a human person. Human DNA is human DNA from the moment of conception, to old age, and even beyond death.

Never is human DNA anything else but human DNA.

We cannot let the use of impressive medical words and terms by pro-abortion voices lead us to believe that an unborn baby is something less than human. Most terms used to refer to an unborn baby are simply false: "globs of miscellaneous tissue," "a sack of tissue," or "a part of a woman's body." Other medical terms, such as *embryo* and *fetus,* are outright misused and misrepresented. While these are real medical terms used to reference an unborn baby, they designate *different stages* of human development, not various levels of humanity. These medical terms, when used in the proper context, simply define the unborn baby's particular stage of life.

From conception onward, the stages of life that represent a maturing human person might go something like this:

- Human zygote
- Human blastocyst
- Human embryo
- Human fetus
- Newborn baby
- Infant
- Toddler
- Child
- Pre-adolescent
- Adolescent
- Adult
- Middle-aged adult
- Mature adult
- Elderly adult

The prefix *human* is simply known to be real. This is the same for a human zygote, human embryo, and human fetus. The prefix *human* should be recognized and acknowledged as known truth. And in every case, no matter what stage of development the unborn baby is in, it is never anything less than a living unborn human baby.

This is the real conversation of life.

About Viability

The Ability to Live

In today's conversation of life, pro-abortion voices have interjected another argument to justify the institution of abortion in America. This argument is so strong that it can effectively justify abortion even if one does recognize and accept the life and humanity of the unborn child.

This argument is viability.

The viability argument holds that if an unborn baby is aborted early enough within a pregnancy, before the point in time when it is sufficiently developed to live outside of the womb, there can be no moral issues to a woman having the abortion. This, pro-abortion voices argue, is because even if the unborn baby is considered by some to be fully alive and fully human *inside* the womb, if this baby is not developed enough to live *outside* the womb, it would die anyway if it were born prematurely.

This, they explain, makes abortion justifiable.

Then, through the slippery slope of pro-abortion thought, if abortions are okay early in a pregnancy, then abortions later in a pregnancy must be fine as well. Besides, they argue, who can tell when life really begins? It's only when the mother says so.

As with the other pro-abortion arguments, in order to make abortion palatable to the American public, the truths regarding unborn life have been dismissed and hidden from view so that the lies and deceptions of the viability argument can be made more believable and acceptable.

In this case, the truth missed by pro-choice voices is that the viability of any organism—that is, the survivability of any organism—is dependent upon one very specific condition for life. This specific condition is *environment.* If any living entity is taken away from the environment in which it is intended in nature to live and grow, and placed in an environment that is not suitable for life, then that living organism will die. This is truth. The organism's ability to survive is directly related to the conditions of the environment in which it is placed.

This same principle applies to an unborn baby. If the unborn baby is taken from the womb of its mother during the time in its life when it is dependent on the environment created by nature inside the womb to live, then that baby will die. The concept of viability presupposes that the only definition of human life that matters is life outside the womb. But more precisely, the concept of viability in relation to the abortion issue dictates that the only definition of life that matters, is life that can survive in an environment only considered as our normal living environment.

We can better see the fallacy of viability, when we apply the same justifications used to justify abortion to other life-or-death situations. Although these scenarios may appear to be senseless and laughable, the application of viability in each case is the same, and with the slippery slope that is the viability argument, the following situations could become more real in today's healthcare climate. With that said, when we apply the issue of viability in a broader sense, at what point would the existing human life of a human person outside the womb, not even matter?

Using the same logic of viability used to justify abortion, the life of any person undergoing open heart surgery would not be considered viable. During this procedure, the heart of this patient is *not* beating, their lungs are *not* functioning, and the patient is *not* openly conscious. In fact, according to pro-abortion logic, this person shouldn't even be considered alive, as open consciousness, a heartbeat, and independent breathing are the three main conditions used by pro-abortion advocates to dismiss the existence of human life within the womb.

The life of the open-heart patient is sustained by the functions of a heart-lung machine, a medical device that oxygenates and distributes the patient's blood throughout the body. This device provides a functional environment necessary for this patient to sustain life during the surgery, much like a mother provides the necessary environment for the unborn baby to sustain life within the womb. However, if you prematurely remove the patient from the heart-lung device, this person will surely die, just as a baby dies if prematurely removed from the life-sustaining environment of its mother's womb.

If we consider the full scope of the viability argument, then this patient's state of non-viability would disqualify him or her from possessing any human rights as guaranteed by the US Constitution. With no rights to life, it would be perfectly legal for an immediate relative to choose to abort this patient's life at any time during the surgery; simply because it would be too mentally distressing, socially inconvenient, or financially overwhelming to bring him back to life. Doctors could be instructed to disconnect this patient prematurely from the heart-lung machine, simply because a next of kin decided that this patient was not healthy enough or intelligent enough to be considered worthy of life.

This happens daily to unborn children.

The same principles of viability would also apply to anybody requiring an oxygen tank to provide sufficient oxygen in the air they breathe to sustain life. Since this person must rely on the environment provided by the oxygen tank to survive, the life of this person must also be considered not viable.

In this case, those saddled with the responsibility to care for the well-being of this non-viable being would have the right to simply deny their responsibility to it, and choose to abort its life, simply because it was a cramp on their lifestyle, got in the way, and/or was simply unwanted. These non-viables could be aborted at any time, especially if nobody wanted to deal with them anymore.

Aborting the life of those considered non-viable and undesired could become something that any viable American citizen could just *do*, like get a haircut or sell their car. The United States Supreme Court could aid in making the termination of these unwanted and undesired non-viable humans socially acceptable and more palatable to American society, simply by dehumanizing them, redefining and reclassifying within the law those who cannot within their own physical means sustain life in our normal environment as a *byproduct of life*.

Unborn children are subject to this standard.

Some of you may remember the boy in the bubble. Born during the 1970s, this young boy had a severe autoimmune disease that made headlines because the only known treatment for his disease was to keep him in a sterile environment—a room-sized plastic bubble. This bubble was like a womb for him and allowed him to live his life as normally as possible. Like an unborn baby within its mother's womb, this young boy could not sustain life outside of this bubble. He lived until the age of twelve.

Wouldn't it have been okay, applying the same line of thinking used to justify early term abortions, for some counselor or expert doctor to have convinced his parents to choose to abort the life of their son, and remove him from the protective bubble that sustained his life, to abort his life at, say, age four, simply because they didn't want to deal with him anymore because his life could become an unnecessary drain on their finances and a burden on their lifestyle? Couldn't they have just taken care of him because they were told that was the right thing to do?

It's okay. He would have died anyway.

*****

The issue of viability was used by the 1973 United States Supreme Court, and strategically placed within the Roe v. Wade ruling, to justifiably dismiss the early stages of the unborn baby's life, to further hide the existence of unborn life and make unborn life more of a non-factor in a mother's choice to have an abortion.

The truth is, all living organisms are designed by nature to mature through time in environments naturally conducive to sustaining life. If any organism is placed in an environment that is not naturally conducive to life, then that organism will die. Unborn human babies are no exception.

A planted flower seed first lives and grows underground for a period of time, developing the root infrastructure it will need for growth and nourishment. Then in the time dictated through nature, the flower plant will emerge from the ground and continue to live and grow in splendid beauty. If the roots are removed from the ground before development is complete, the plant loses its ability to metabolize energy. The flower plant will die. Like a human baby within the womb, it's not that the flower plant was never alive while underground, out of the sight of the human eye. The flower plant, like a human baby, is simply designed by nature to live, grow, and mature in one environment, before being born from that initial place and further flourishing in another.

This is the real conversation of life.

About Recognizing

To Realize or Perceive Something as Existing or True

I t was just after Christmas, and I had just returned to school following a family trip to Florida during the break. I remember as if it were yesterday…

I was in the second grade, participating in a class spelling bee. One half of the class lined up on the left side of the classroom, the other half on the right, one side against the other; the last person standing would win the honor of victory for his or her side. I knew my odds. I didn't have any grand illusions about being the last one standing. I just didn't want to go out in the first round.

I stood in the middle of the line, anxiously awaiting my turn. My anxiety level grew as one by one the words came down the line. Some of the words I knew, others I didn't. Energy shot up and down my spine, my posture straightened tighter and tighter as the words headed my way. Finally, it was my turn.

"Jeff, spell the word, *through*," my teacher said.

All anxiety left me. A picture of the word instantly popped into my head.

Confidently I began the spelling, "T-H-R-U." I paused for a moment. A muffled giggle sounded from the other side of the room. My confidence quickly eroded. Another muffled giggle crossed the room. The pressure was on, yet the image of the word remained imprinted in the forefront of my mind. *It must be right,* I thought, *it has to be right,* "T-H-R-U, thru," I quickly repeated.

"No, that is not correct," my teacher told me. "Please sit down in your seat."

The little giggle turned into a demeaning laugh.

I was shocked. "What do you mean?" I questioned, not understanding why.

"You didn't spell the word correctly."

"But that's how I saw it! That's the way it's spelled on the traffic signs," I pleaded my case. "That's the way it's spelled. I saw it. I saw the signs. It's spelled that way all the way to Florida and back."

My teacher raised an eyebrow, tilted her head slightly, and then paused for a moment. It felt like an eternity. Only a couple of kids were sitting down, and I wasn't liking the idea of joining them, especially this early in the contest. Somewhere deep inside, I knew that the way I spelled the word didn't sound right. But that was how I saw it, and I saw it so many times I couldn't come up with any other way. *It has to be at least a little bit right, at least enough to stay in line,* I thought. Through that small piece of eternity, I racked my brain attempting to recall a different way to spell the word, but to no avail. All that I could picture was "thru" as I had seen it probably hundreds of times on the highway traffic signs.

"I'm sorry," she finally said. "That is not the correct spelling. Please take your seat."

My jaw dropped, along with my shoulders and head. An audible, protesting, "Huh" sounded past my lips. I went to my desk and slumped into my seat. I was embarrassed. *How can it be wrong? It is spelled like that all over the place.* I felt like I had been tricked.

My teacher must have seen that I was upset. "I'm sorry, but you have to know what's right, so you can better recognize when something is wrong."

About Verity

Conforming to Reality or Actuality

America has spent decades arguing over whether or not we *feel* or *believe* an unborn baby is alive within the womb. We have stood across the line on the playground, we have thrown our old clichés and phrases back and forth, over and over again. If we haven't been actively involved in this clash of feelings and beliefs, we have taunted and jeered from the middle. This is the conversation of life in America. The conversation is the same as it has always been, nothing has changed.

But today's conversation of life is wrong. Unborn human life exists from the moment of conception. This is more than just a religious belief or personal perception; this is fact. This is medical truth. This is scientific law, universally recognized as true forever and always, just like the law of gravity. There is no sense in trying to argue otherwise.

Now we must turn our attention to abortion itself. What is an abortion? What happens to the unborn human life during the abortion process?

If we weren't so preoccupied with arguing over whether unborn human life exists in the first place, we could have gone right to the most straightforward approach and simply looked up abortion in a medical dictionary and found the answer not only to abortion, but unborn human life. Here we find that the *Merriam-Webster Medical Dictionary* defines an abortion as:

> The termination of a pregnancy after, accompanied by, resulting in, or closely followed by the death of the embryo or fetus.

The termination of a pregnancy. The death of the unborn baby. And we know, for there to be death, there must first have been life.

This is the real conversation of life.

Right there is everything we need to know about abortion in one quick, easy-to-read and understandable definition. But we are a stubborn nation, and so many of us must insist that answers to such a volatile issue as abortion cannot be that simple, cannot be that straightforward. So we must go deeper.

*****

Pregnancy is a conditional medical diagnosis. That is, for a woman to be medically diagnosed as pregnant, there must be a certain condition; she must have within her a living baby. The living unborn baby is the *condition* that defines a woman as pregnant. Once a woman has become pregnant, the only way for her to not be pregnant *anymore* is when the unborn baby is not within her *anymore*.

There are only three scenarios in which a pregnant woman can become not pregnant anymore.

First: The living baby could die naturally while still within the womb, in which in time the mother will naturally expel the baby. This is called a miscarriage. The woman is not pregnant anymore.

Second: The living unborn baby could be delivered from the womb alive and be born into this world. This is called a live birth. The woman is not pregnant anymore.

Third: A pregnant woman can choose to have an abortion, and then not be pregnant anymore.

*****

In performing this certain abortion procedure, the pregnant mother is prepared to deliver her baby in much the same way as any other induced labor and delivery, with the administration of drugs that will cause her cervix to dilate, and in some cases, induce contractions. Once the cervix is sufficiently dilated, the doctor will intentionally situate the baby in the womb so that it will travel through the birth canal breach or backward, feet first. If the contractions caused by the medications are not strong enough to naturally push the baby through the birth canal, the doctor will manually assist the baby out by reaching up into the woman's uterus to grab the legs of the baby with his/her hand or a long medical instrument, and then pull the baby through the birth canal. The feet will come through first, then the legs, the torso, the arms, and the shoulders. Once the head reaches the cervix, however, the baby is stopped by the doctor from proceeding any further.

At this point, it's important to understand that should the head of this baby come out past the cervix, the baby, then completely outside of its mother, would be medically and legally considered to be fully delivered. The baby was alive within its mother, and the baby, now outside the womb of its mother, will still be alive. This baby would be legally born, legally classified as a live birth.

If this baby is born alive, then there is a legal and moral responsibility to keep the baby alive. But this is an abortion procedure; the woman doesn't want her baby. She just doesn't want to be pregnant anymore. Should a live birth occur, the abortion procedure would have failed.

Since the intention of an abortion procedure is to relieve the mother of her unwanted baby, so she will not be pregnant anymore, a live birth cannot occur. Therefore, the doctor, while still holding the baby's head within the cervix, will palpitate the base of the baby's skull to locate a spot where the bone tissue is the softest. Once this spot has been located, he/she will use a razor sharp medical instrument to pierce a hole into the back of the baby's head, through the skull, and deep into the brain tissue. After successfully creating a pathway into the center of the baby's head, the doctor will remove the instrument, insert a special suctioning needle, then proceed to extract the baby's brain tissue. As the brain of this baby is being sucked out, the pressure from the cervix collapses its skull. With no brain and a collapsed skull, this unborn baby is now dead.

This baby, seconds earlier fully alive in its mother's womb, seconds away from breathing its first breath in this world, seconds away from being held lovingly in someone's arms, seconds away from the opportunity to grow up—to love, and to be loved—has been intentionally killed by the doctor.

Now that the baby is dead, the doctor can finally fully deliver the lifeless baby from its mother, cut the umbilical cord, and deposit the baby to be destroyed as medical waste. Nothing more than a byproduct of conception.

The abortion procedure has been a success. The mother is no longer pregnant. The unwanted baby has been taken care of.

*****

This revelation regarding the horrific truths of abortion may come as a shock, almost too gruesome to be true. Yet there are court transcripts from a Senate Judiciary Committee hearing in March of 1996 that confirm the brutality of this procedure. This following testimony was given by an operating nurse who witnessed an abortion doctor perform this exact procedure on a twenty-six-and-a-half-week-old baby within the womb:

> Dr. Haskell went in with forceps and grabbed the baby's legs and pulled them down into the birth canal. Then he delivered the baby's body and the arms—everything but the head. The doctor kept the head right inside the uterus...
>
> The baby's little fingers were clasping and unclasping, and his little feet were kicking. Then the doctor stuck the scissors in the back of his head, and the baby's arms jerked out, like a startle reaction, like a flinch, like a baby does when he thinks he is going to fall.

The doctor opened up the scissors, stuck a high-powered suction tube into the opening, and sucked the baby's brains out. Now the baby went completely limp…

He cut the umbilical cord and delivered the placenta. He threw the baby in a pan, along with the placenta and the instruments he had just used.

Statement of Brenda Pratt Shafer, RN
Before the Subcommittee on the Constitution
Committee of the Judiciary
US House of Representatives
Hearing on the Partial Birth
Abortion Act (HR1833)
March 21, 1996

You have heard of this procedure before. You know this procedure as partial birth abortion.

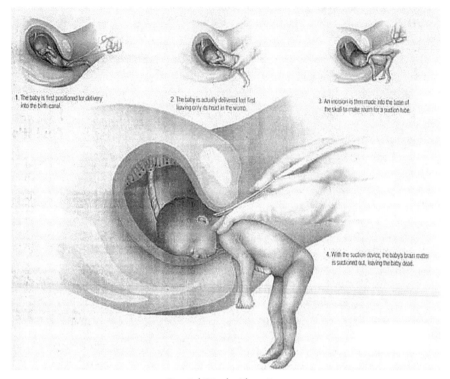

1. The baby is first positioned for delivery into the birth canal.

2. The baby is actually delivered feet first leaving only its head in the womb.

3. An incision is then made into the base of the skull to make room for a suction tube.

4. With the suction device, the baby's brain matter is suctioned out, leaving the baby dead.

Partial Birth Abortion

This is the real picture of abortion.

The descriptions of the medical procedures, legal testimony, and images of this abortion procedure absolutely describe, without question, the undeniable realities of abortion. The unborn baby is alive within the womb of its mother. The unborn baby is intentionally killed by the doctor. Then, assured the unborn baby is indeed dead, the doctor finally physically removes the baby from its mother.

These are the medical truths of abortion. These are the medical truths of *all* abortions.

*****

You must remember that there is a legal aspect to life and death in America. Within every aspect of our laws, science in its relation to medicine, and medicine in its relation to science, especially when human life and death is involved, must be completely understood, specified, and fully defined. This careful attention to the relationship between law, science, and medicine must exist to assure that every legal, moral, and ethical challenge to the law can not only be determined but be well understood, specified, and wholly defined.

This might be difficult to believe, but the gruesome realities of abortion—that the unborn baby is alive, and that the unborn baby is intentionally killed before being removed from the womb of its mother—are also found *specifically defined and confirmed within the very wording of United States law.* As written within the Partial Birth Abortion Act signed into law by President George W. Bush in 2003, a partial-birth abortion is legally defined within United States federal law as an abortion in which:

> (A) the person performing the abortion delib-
> erately and intentionally vaginally delivers a
> living fetus until, in the case of a head-first
> presentation, the entire fetal head is out-
> side the body of the mother, or, in the case
> of breech presentation, any part of the fetal
> trunk past the navel is outside the body of
> the mother for the purpose of performing an
> overt act that the person knows will kill the
> partially delivered living fetus; and
>
> (B) performs the overt act, other than comple-
> tion of delivery, that kills the partially deliv-
> ered living fetus;

This is the legal definition of an abortion, as it is written within the federal law of the United States: "An overt act that…the person knows will kill the…living fetus."

President George W. Bush banned partial birth abortion in 2003, and this ban was upheld by the Supreme Court in 2006. Although this particular abortion procedure has been federally ruled illegal, there are many other abortion procedures a doctor can choose, each one just as brutal, each one perfectly legal. All abortion procedures follow the same precepts: that the unborn baby is alive, the unborn baby is intentionally killed while still within its mother, and then forcibly removed.

Now we know why Justice Sotomayor didn't say anything in reference to the well-promoted pro-abortion platform: "The unborn baby isn't alive. It's what you believe; it's just a woman's choice." She couldn't state the standard pro-abortion platforms that we are inundated with day in and day out by the pro-abortion media and present them as truth, because they are all nothing but lies and deceptions.

*****

Again, we are a stubborn nation, and some of us need additional proof. Proof that the unborn baby is alive. Proof that the unborn baby is intentionally killed through an abortion procedure.

Following are testimony excerpts from official federal court transcripts. These transcripts are a matter of public record and depict the testimonies of doctors under oath of truth as they describe for the US district courts of New York, Nebraska, and California, the realities of abortion.

In the transcripts, "Q" indicates questions from the lawyers, and "A" indicates answers from the abortion provider or doctor on the witness stand. These answers will appear in italics. Occasionally you will see "The Court," designating questions or comments that came directly from the presiding justice. "The Witness" is the doctor or abortion provider on the witness stand who answers the justice's question.

To assure accurateness and clarity, the doctor's name, the district court hearing the case, the case name, transcript page number, and date of testimony have been provided. Typographical errors are the result of the actual transcript.

First, we'll begin with testimony describing some additional methods of abortion. This is what an actual abortion provider testified regarding three available options to terminate a late-term pregnancy.

> **Q: One method [of terminating a late-term pregnancy] would be to pull on the baby so that the head breaks off from the rest of the body; is that right?**
> *A: Yes.*
>
> **Q And then, you would go inside the uterus and remove the head?**
> *A: Correct.*
>
> **Q: The next method is that you would use scissors to puncture the base of the skull?**
> *A: Correct.*
>
> **Q: And then, you will stick a suction cannula into the opening and drain the brain tissue?**
> *A: Did you say "Drain the brain tissue"?*
>
> **Q: Then you drain the brain tissue?**
> *A: Yes.*
>
> **Q: And the third method is that you take a crushing instrument, put that instrument inside...crush the baby's head, and pull the head through the cervix, correct?**
> *A: That would be a third possible...those are my three options...*

Dr. Mitchell Creinin
Planned Parenthood v. Ashcroft
US District Court, Northern District of California
pp. 745–746
April 6, 2004

These are descriptions of three different types of late-term abortions. Of note, only the procedure where the baby is partially delivered and the brain sucked out, known as partial birth abortion because the majority of the baby is outside the woman's body when it is killed, has been banned. The others remain completely legal. Further testimonies reveal the details of the other legal late-term abortion procedures.

Q: So moving along, once you've located and grasped the lower extremities and turn the fetus if you need to, what do you do next?
A: Pull with the instrument that I am using to remove the fetus with the attempt to remove the fetus in as few passes as possible...

Q: Why?
A: The fetus will either continue to come or will begin to break apart. It will break apart wherever or whatever it is. It may be in the middle of the leg, it may be in the abdomen, it may be in the chest...

Dr. Mitchell Creinin
Planned Parenthood v Ashcroft
US District Court, Northern
District of California
p. 678
April 5, 2004

Q: And what's your next step, at that point, if the fetus has lodged at the cervical os [opening]?
A:...I would use a forcep...remove the part of [the] fetus that was easily reachable. Hopefully try to use small bites to work the way up and remove the rest of the fetus so that it comes out intact. If not, then remove whatever part that I could get easily and then go back and remove the rest.

Dr. Leroy Carhart
Leroy Carhart et al. v Ashcroft
US District Court, District of Nebraska
pp. 617–618
April 1, 2004

Q: All right. Going back now, I think you said in some instances when you use a suction cannula, that part of the fetus or the umbilical cord will come out through the cervix. Then what do you do at that point?
A: Well, if the umbilical cord comes down, I unattach that from its integrity. I just break it and pull on it. If a foot comes down, I grab the foot and pull down on that.

Q: If no part comes down, as a result of the suction, what do you do?
A: Then I have to place the ring forceps up into the uterus and find a part.

Q: And is there a particular part that you're trying to grasp, at that point?
A: I take whatever I can get, because I have really—I have a feel of when you feel the cranium of the head, but that's about the only thing I have a feel of

when you grasp until you pull it down... I just pull down with the forceps and, you know, see what part you have, and see if you can get more of that part out. If you get more of the part out, you twist to try to get more tissue out. If that doesn't happen, then you pull hard enough that it will disarticulate at that point or break off at that point.

Dr. William Fitzhugh:
Leroy Carhart et al. v. Ashcroft
US District Court, District of Nebraska
p. 240
March 30, 2004

The transcript excerpts you have just read detail a *dismemberment method* of abortion. With this method, the cervix is dilated so that the doctor can reach up into the woman's uterus with either fingers or a medical instrument to dismember—literally tear apart the baby—pulling it from the mother, piece by piece. Each time a body part comes out is called a *pass,* and it can take up to fifteen or twenty passes to fully remove the baby's body parts, placenta, and membranes.

The following excerpts detail a different version of late-term abortion:

The Court: Can you explain to me what that means?
The Witness: What they did was they delivered the fetus intact until the head was still trapped behind the cervix, and then they reached up and crushed the head in order to deliver it through the cervix.

The Court: What did they utilize to crush the head?
The Witness: An instrument, a large pair of forceps that have a round, serrated edge at the end of it, so

that they were able to bring them together and crush the head between the ends of the instrument.

Dr. Timothy Johnson
National Abortion Federation et al. v. Ashcroft
US District Court,
Southern District of New York
pp. 466–467
March 31, 2004

Q: What actions do you take during a D&E that would be fatal to the fetus?
A: Well, number one, I like to interrupt the umbilical cord. Number two, we are working on a young gestation, but that's not to do it. And we break up parts in the uterus and we crush skulls.

Dr. William Fitzhugh
Leroy Carhart et al. v. Ashcroft
US District Court, District of Nebraska
p. 253
March 30, 2004

Q: Dr. Chasen, in your experience, how is the fetal head extracted in a dismemberment D&E?
A: The fetal head is extracted by placing forceps around it and crushing it.

These transcripts described a method used by doctors to kill the unborn baby during the abortion procedure, by crushing its head with a medical instrument not unlike a large pair of pliers.

There is another dismemberment method used by doctors to kill and remove the unborn baby during an abortion procedure. In this method, the unborn baby is truly beheaded, killed when the doctor reaches up and breaks off the baby's head, disconnecting it from the rest of its body.

> **Q: In those cases in which you are doing a D&E and the fetus delivers partially intact except for the calvarium [the baby's head] getting stuck in the cervix, you have to insert forceps and crush the calvarium; is that right?**
> *A: I would separate the caldarium [the baby's head] from the fetal—how I would perform the procedure is, I would separate the caldarium from the fetal body, thorax, and then insert the forceps to crush the caldarium to be able to deliver it.*

Dr. "Doe" (testifying under a pseudonym)
Planned Parenthood v. Ashcroft
US District Court,
Northern District of California
p. 33
April 1, 2004

> **Q: One method would be to pull on the baby so that the head breaks off from the rest of the body; is that right?**
> *A: Yes.*

> **Q: And that would ensure that you did not deliver a live baby?**
> *A: Correct.*

Dr. Mitchell Creinin
Planned Parenthood v Ashcroft
U.S. District Court,
Northern District of California
p. 745
April 6, 2004

Then there is the question of life. The popular media has led us to believe for decades that the baby isn't alive within the womb, that determining the presence of unborn life is above our pay grade. Yet we know now that science, medicine, and the law all definitively state the baby is fully alive within its mother's womb from the moment of conception. Let these testimonies from real abortion doctors confirm what we already know to be true regarding the life and death relationship between the unborn baby and abortion.

Q: And when you begin the evacuation, is the fetus ever alive?
A: Yes.

Q: You testified earlier, Dr. Paul, that the fetus can be alive when the evacuation begins; is that correct?
A: That's right.

Q: When in the course of the abortion does the fetus—does fetal demise occur?
A: I don't know for sure. I certainly know that if I deliver intact and collapse the skull that demise occurs.

Dr. Maureen Paul
Planned Parenthood v. Ashcroft
US District Court,
Northern District of California
pp. 67, 73
March 29, 2004

Q: But some of them [the babies] are alive at the time you do the procedure?
A: The majority of them are alive at the time.

Dr. William Fitzhugh
Leroy Carhart et al. v. Ashcroft
US District Court, District of Nebraska
p. 252
March 30, 2004

Q: Doctor, if a woman's cervix was so dilated the fetus could be delivered in intact it would not be necessary to collapse the skull because the fetus could pass through the cervix, right?
A: Correct.

Q: But you would not allow the fetus to pass intact...?
A: Correct.

Q: Because if the fetus were close to 24 weeks, and you were performing a transvaginal surgical abortion you would be concerned about delivering the fetus entirely intact because that might result in a live baby that may survive, correct?
A: You said I was performing an abortion, so since the objective of the abortion is to not have a live fetus, then that would be correct.

Dr. Mitchell Creinin
Planned Parenthood v. Ashcroft
US District Court,
Northern District of California
pp. 747–748
April 6, 2004

The real outcome of abortion, the intended outcome of an abortion procedure, says a lot about the issue. What is the real outcome of a woman's right to choose? The true intent, the true goal of the physician during an abortion procedure, regardless of the pain caused by method used to put the baby to death, is disclosed in the following testimony.

Q: Dr. Weiss, what is your purpose, in the example you just gave, in delivering the fetus up to the head and removing an arm? What is your purpose in doing that?
A: Your purpose in doing the procedure is overall to terminate the pregnancy, to make the woman no longer pregnant.

Dr. Gerson Weiss
National Abortion Federation et al. v. Ashcroft
US District Court, Southern District of New York
p. 1363
April 7, 2004

Q: And one step you would take to avoid delivery of a live baby would to be to deliver or hold the fetus' head on the internal side of the cervical os in order to collapse the skull; is that right?
A: Yes, because the objective of my procedure is to perform an abortion.

Q: And that would ensure that you did not deliver a live baby?
A: Correct.

Dr. Mitchell Creinin
Planned Parenthood v. Ashcroft
US District Court, Northern District of California
p. 748
April 6, 2004

The Court: Excuse me. You don't feel any obligation whatsoever to protect the life of the fetus?
The Witness: We are seeing—

The Court: I am asking you something.
The Witness: With many of my patients, yes, particularly post-viability, your Honor.

The Court: You don't find any dual responsibility; your obligation is only to the woman?
The Witness: In the circumstances in which I am doing terminations, that is correct.

Dr. Cassing Hammond
National Abortion Federation et al. v. Ashcroft
US District Court, Southern District of New York
pp. 38–39
April 1, 2004

Q: Doctor, in earlier answer, again I think in response to a question put to you by his honor, you made reference to certain observations you have made concerning fetal response to stimuli and response to anesthesia; what were those observations?
A: In some cases prior to inserting [laminaria] and performing the abortion procedure I will do a procedure to effect fetal death. I will inject the fetus with potassium which will stop the heart. The most common way to do this is by injecting a fetal directly into the heart of the fetus under ultrasound guidance. Now these cases the mothers are not anesthetized and the fetuses don't receive any anesthesia by route of the mother. And in every one of these cases, upon contact of the needle with the fetal chest, I see

a withdrawal response of the fetus, recoiling that I can see on the ultrasound.

Dr. Stephen T. Chasen
National Abortion Federation et al. v. Ashcroft
US District Court, Southern District of New York
p. 76
April 8, 2004

The Court: Simple question, Doctor. Does it cross your mind?
The Witness: Does the fetus having pain cross your mind?

The Court: Yes.
The Witness: No.

The Court: Never crossed your mind.
The Witness: No.

Dr. Timothy Johnson
National Abortion Federation et al. v. Ashcroft
US District Court, Southern District of New York
p. 513
March 31, 2004

Q: Dr. Chasen, in your experience, how is the fetal head extracted in a dismemberment D&E?
A: The fetal head is extracted by placing forceps around it and crushing it.

Q: Does it hurt the baby?
A: I don't know.

Q: But you go ahead and do it anyway, right?
A: I am taking care of my patients, and in that process, yes, I go ahead and do it.

The Court: Does that mean that you take care of your patient and the baby be damned, is that the approach you have?
The Witness: These women who are having [abortions] at gestational ages they are legally entitled to it—

The Court: I didn't ask you that, doctor. I asked if you had any caring or concern for the fetus whose head you were crushing.
The Witness: No.

Dr. Chasen
National Abortion Federation et al. v. Ashcroft
US District Court, Southern District of New York
pp. 101–102
April 8, 2004

Medical necessity, the idea that abortions are necessary to assure that the pregnancy does not harm the health of the mother, is another argument used to promote abortion. But is it really necessary? The American College of Obstetricians and Gynecologists has their position on this issue. This is what was testified in accordance with the medical necessity argument.

Q: And, Doctor, what is your opinion concerning the medical necessity of partial-birth abortion procedures such as intact D&E with regard to preserving the health of the mother?
A: Well, I will restate what the American College of Obstetricians and Gynecologists said in their statement. They know of no instance where it's necessary

to use this procedure to—they could think of no specific instance when this procedure would be necessary to protect the health of the mother.

Dr. Watson Bowes, Jr.
Leroy Carhart et al. v. Ashcroft
US District Court, District of Nebraska
p. 988
April 5, 2004

Q: When a pregnancy has to be ended prematurely, because of a maternal health condition of the kind that you treat, is it ever necessary to take a destructive act against the fetus directly, in order to protect the health interests of the mother?
A: No, all that is required for recovery of the mother is for separation of the fetus and placenta from her system so that she can start the recovery process. There is nothing inherent in the destruction of the fetus that starts to facilitate that process.

Dr. Curtis Cook
Leroy Carhart et al. v. Ashcroft
US District Court, District of Nebraska
p. 1306
April 7, 2004

Q: So you have never encountered a situation where the pregnancy had to be terminated before viability because of a maternal health condition?
A: I have not.

Q: Doctor, are you aware of any maternal health conditions that would require terminating pregnancy by the intact D&X method?
A: And after careful review and after sitting on both the ACOG—correction—AMA task force, we could not find any medical conditions that would require an intact D&X. The ACOG panel could not come up with any situations that would require an intact D&X....

Q: Doctor, in your practice have you seen a need for the use of the intact D&X method?
A: I have never seen a situation where an intact D&X method was necessary to be performed.

Dr. M. Leroy Sprang
Planned Parenthood v. Ashcroft
US District Court, Northern District of California
pp. 1109–1111
April 9, 2004

*****

Real abortion truths, from real abortion doctors:

> *You take a crushing instrument, put that instrument inside...crush the baby's head, and pull the head through the cervix...*
>
> *The fetus will either continue to come or will begin to break apart. It will break apart wherever or whatever it is. It may be in the middle of the leg, it may be at the abdomen, it may be at the chest...*
>
> *You said I was performing an abortion, so since the objective of the abortion is to not have a live fetus...*

Normally…the fetuses are alive at the time of the final delivery.

I will do a procedure to effect fetal death. I will inject the fetus with potassium which will stop the heart. The most common way to do this is by injecting a needle directly into the heart of the fetus… And in every one of these cases, upon contact of the needle with the fetal chest, I see a withdrawal response of the fetus, recoiling that I can see on the ultrasound.

The intent of an [abortion is] that the fetus will die during the process…

*****

These are just some of the many testimonies taken from the hundreds of pages of transcripts of the United States Federal Courts participating in this case. These testimonies reveal in tragic detail the truth, the whole truth, and nothing but the truth—the gruesome, sad, horrible truths of abortion; truths that are not just believed to be true, but known to be true.

Through these transcripts, we see the real grotesque truths of abortion. We find that an unborn baby is *fully alive* before an abortion procedure, and then *intentionally killed* in the process of an abortion procedure. These unborn babies are *viable, human, and capable of surviving* if the pregnancy would be allowed to go to term.

We find that there is a *total disregard for the type of death* the baby incurs—death by dismemberment, beheading, crushing of head, etc. There are no obligations, no "human rights," or any rights for that matter, offered toward the baby. Plus, we now know that unborn babies *can, and do,* feel the pain of being killed during the abortion. And the justification of medical necessity, the go-to excuse for legislators to deny the passing of abortion restricting laws, isn't truly a justifiable reason for abortion.

Yet every single one of these truths, every single one of these realities depicting and defining abortion, are adamantly denied as real by the pro-abortion voices of pro-choice advocates and the popular media.

In the United States courtroom, there are just facts. Notice that within these courtroom transcripts, there is no debate on whether the baby is alive, no discussions of one's philosophies, ideologies, or theologies toward unborn life. The objective fact is that the unborn baby is alive within the mother, from conception. Notice there is no argument on whether the unborn baby is truly a human baby. It's not a thing, some precursor to becoming a human baby. There is just courtroom fact; unborn human babies are always considered living human babies. Notice that there is no discussion on *any* of the topics you and I hear when abortion is talked about publicly. All we find are the courtroom facts of how, when, and why the unborn baby is killed within its mother during an abortion procedure.

This is the real conversation of life.

*****

Truth can be disturbing. Truth can be shocking. Truth can be upsetting. Yet, no matter what the emotional result of realizing truth is, truth always remains *truth*. Truth always depicts *reality*. Through the revelations recorded for public access within these court transcripts, our pictures of unborn life and abortion have become very different. The transcripts we have just reviewed describe only a few of the methods a doctor may choose from to perform an abortion. There are numerous other procedures available to kill the unborn baby, each one perfectly legal, and each one incredibly barbaric.

In some abortions, the baby is killed and removed from its mother by manually inserting a syringe into the uterus and sucking the baby out. This is medically referred to as MVA, or manual vacuum aspiration. The baby can also be killed and removed using a small electric vacuum, medically known as EVA, electric vacuum aspiration. During these procedures, the baby is effectively ripped apart and sucked from the mother's uterus, piece by piece.

Another common method is called dilation and curettage, or sharp curettage. This procedure uses a long medical instrument with a sharp, spoon-shaped knife at the end. Once inserted into the woman's uterus and turned on, the rapidly spinning blade cuts, tears apart, and scrapes the baby out from the interior of the mother's uterus.

In some abortions, a lethally toxic solution is injected into the amniotic fluid that surrounds the baby. Externally, this toxic solution chemically burns the outside tissues of the baby, that of the eyes and skin. However, it isn't this chemical burning of the external soft tissue that causes the baby to die. This procedure causes death when the baby drinks this highly toxic amniotic fluid and ingests it into its digestive system. This poisoned fluid attacks and burns the soft tissue and membranes within the baby's mouth, throat, esophagus, stomach, and intestines, initiating a slow burning of these internal tissues, eventually causing seizures, hemorrhaging, and over the course of several hours, or even days, the eventual death of the baby.

Lethal injection is also used a different way, in a different abortion procedure. In this case, the doctor injects a highly toxic substance by way of needle and syringe directly into the chest cavity of the baby, or even better according to abortion doctors, directly into its beating heart. The objective of this abortion procedure, obviously, is to stop the baby's heart from beating, to kill the unborn baby.

In either of these procedures, once the baby is killed, labor is induced, and the baby delivered, dead on arrival.

The abortion procedure has been a success. The mother is not pregnant anymore.

Then there are the countless millions of children who were denied the continuation of life through the morning-after or plan B pill, which doesn't allow a newly formed human embryo to attach to the uterus of its mother. Also uncounted are the millions of newly formed babies created in a petri dish for the purpose of invitro fertilization, whose lives are suspended indefinitely in a frozen laboratory environment. These unused embryos face being medically discarded as byproducts of conception or used as specimens in medical stem cell research.

Sadly, we live in a world where what the politician said is true, the unborn baby is only alive—when the mother says so.

When the mother says so...

Killed at 7weeks. Suction method

Killed at 18 weeks. Lethal saline injection
Note burnt skin.

Hand and foot of 14 week old aborted
baby. Suction method.

Aborted babies.
Killed at
24 weeks
21 weeks

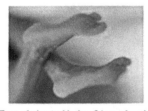

Feet of aborted baby. 21 weeks old.

Twins. Killed at 12 weeks.
Suction method

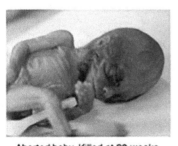

Aborted baby. Killed at 20 weeks

All photos courtesy of
Citizens for a Pro-Life Society
www.imagesofabortion.org

24 week old baby
Killed by D and E abortion
Dismemberment method

Hand of aborted baby.
21 weeks old.

The New Conversation of Life

The True Pictures of Abortion

We live in a society today that justifies the legality of abortion by allowing us to define for ourselves the existence of unborn human life. There is no knowledge of truth in today's conversation of life to help us form our conscience toward abortion. Instead, we are told that we can decide for ourselves whether we want the unborn baby to be alive or not alive, human or nonhuman, a real baby or a glob of blood and tissue; that we can use these perceptions to decide whether we want abortion to be good or bad; and that we can paint in the remaining details of our portrait using the colors of our own individual subjective beliefs, perspectives, philosophies, attitudes, and prejudices toward the issue. Through today's pro-abortion conversation of life, we are left to paint our own pictures of abortion by ourselves, for ourselves, without the benefit of knowing the truth. What we end up with is a vague, abstract, self-conceived concept of abortion. And as with anything self-conceived and abstract, we can learn only what we allow ourselves to see. That is—only what we personally *want* to see.

These are *real* images of abortion. These images reflect the tragic and gruesome realities of a woman's choice to end her pregnancy—unborn life brutally destroyed while within the otherwise protective wombs of their mother. These images aren't anything like the abstract portraits today's pro-abortion-driven conversation of life wants us to paint, and not what anyone wants to see. But each one of these images reflect the truths of abortion. And if we are to have a viewpoint of abortion, we must see abortion through the eyes of reality and truth.

*****

A long habit of not thinking abortion as wrong has given it the superficial appearance of being right. The lies and deceptions of abortion have been made right in America for almost five decades. Through the societal cloaking of truth behind the lies and deceptions of today's pro-abortion conversation, innocent unborn children have been shredded, dismembered, and poisoned within the womb because their mother was assured that it was the right thing to do: an unwanted baby taken care of, an unintended pregnancy easily hidden, inappropriate sexual activity effectively veiled. We have come to view abortion as just some "thing" that girls can do, like have periods, pierce their ears, or shave their legs—an available appointment that keeps a girl out of trouble with her parents, boyfriend, or husband. Unborn children are seen as nothing more than a glob of tissue and blood, just part of a woman's body, nothing at all like a real human baby. Unborn life has become a joke, outrightly denied by pro-abortion politicians and advocates. We are assured that abortion has nothing to do with an unborn baby. It's all about a woman's choice, the embodiment of a woman's reproductive right, "a matter of settled law."

We have moved so far into this world of wrong, promoted as a "right," that recognizing the difference between what's truly right and what's truly wrong is nearly impossible. All attempts to help women come to know, understand, and respect the life of their unborn child, as well as realize the inherent dignity they possess in their ability to bear children, are met with aggravation, insensitivity, anger, and censor. Anyone who voices an opposing position to abortion is quickly labeled as close-minded, mean-spirited, and draconian—accused of hate and intolerance.

At the same time, the voices of pro-abortion forces actively promoting the lies and deceptions of unborn life and abortion are amplified and reverberated as truth and reality throughout society. Through the power and influence of the pro-abortion popular media, these voices that intentionally mislead the American public into accepting and promoting the brutal killing of a living unborn human baby are considered the compassionate, understanding, and virtuous voices of abortion, voices representing the benefit and good of all women and society.

Lies and deceptions are promoted as truth, real truths advertised to be lies. Objective truth has become wayward individual perception; false perceptions are recognized as objective truth. Right is promoted as wrong. Wrong is promoted as a "right." Truth and love are left unrecognizable; fear and hatred toward the unborn child is demanded.

Can you now recognize this for what it is? This is evil. True evil. Evil tells us that right is wrong. Evil rejects truth. Rejects love. This is how evil works. This is how the evils of abortion have permeated deeply into American society.

We've been led for decades to see the evils of abortion as morally acceptable, beneficial, and even virtuous for women and society. We've been tricked into believing that abortion is all about the financial, social, and mental difficulties of a pregnant woman. We have been enlightened that abortion has nothing to do with an unborn baby. We have been educated by our own "ministers of public enlightenment and propaganda" to believe that some unborn children are not alive, not human, or simply not worthy of life—should the mother say so.

We began this book with a journey toward truth. We started in the ignorance, confusion, and darkness created by today's pro-abortion conversation of life. We shared in the hurt of a young lady, whose realization of life and love came too late. We recognized that even through disbelief, the miracle of unborn life and childbirth could be realized. Then as we journeyed further toward objective truth— toward the truths of nature, science, medicine, and even United States law—the light of truth gradually replaced the darkness of evil. Then finally, through full recognition of truth in the highest courts of the United States and firsthand examination of real images of abortion, we fully recognized in ultimate clarity the truth of life. The truth of love.

Our hearts, our minds, our lives should never be the same.

*****

Now that we fully see and recognize the truth and realities of abortion, let's look at another presidential debate, this one in 2016, to see the reality of today's conversation of life. In this exchange, Republican candidate Donald Trump commented on a question regarding late-term partial-birth abortion with the following statements:

> Well, I think it's terrible... In the ninth month, you can take the baby and rip the baby out of the womb of the mother just prior to the birth of the baby.
>
> Now you can say that that's okay, and Hillary can say that that's okay. But it's not okay with me, because based on what she's saying and based on where she's going and where she's been, you can take the baby and rip the baby out of the womb in the ninth month on the final day. And that's not acceptable.

In response, Democratic candidate Hillary Clinton had the following to say:

> Well, that is not what happens in these cases. And using that kind of scare rhetoric is just terribly unfortunate.

And the pro-abortion media had their part in this conversation. This is the response of the debate moderator when Mr. Trump wished to counter her statement...

> All right. But just briefly, I want to move on to another segment...

In this clear representation of today's conversation of life, Mr. Trump spoke the truth of abortion. And as normal, this truth was presented by the media as nothing more than the misled superfluous hyperbole of a Republican candidate trying to stand up for his just-as-misled pro-life voting base. Then pro-abortion candidate Hillary Clinton simply lies and denies the truth, denouncing it as nothing other than a scare tactic. This deception by Ms. Clinton was promoted and recognized within society as truth. And the pro-abortion media played along with Ms. Clinton by not offering a truthful correction to her deception and lies; let's just move along.

And thousands of unborn children have been brutally killed since. Go back and look at the images. Thousands upon thousands of innocent human babies, roughly three thousand *per day*, are now dead as a result of that conversation and those that have followed.

This is the pro-abortion conversation of life. Every time we hear this rhetoric, we should now picture the images of an aborted child. Every time we read or hear pro-abortion propaganda, we can now recall the descriptions of abortion we know are used by doctors for each procedure. Every time we hear an unborn baby coldly referenced as only an *embryo, fetus,* or *just part of a woman's body*, we should think of other hurtful words used to dehumanize humanity such as *nigger* or similar derogatory reference toward *Jews*. Knowing the truth, who cannot be sickened by these pro-abortion lies and deceptions? How can anyone with full knowledge of truth stand back and let this evil conversation continue?

*****

To be *born* means to be brought forth. From the realization and acceptance of truth and love in our hearts, a new abortion conversation will be born—a new *Conversation of Life.*

Let us bring forth this new conversation—one that promotes a new understanding, respect, and protection for all unborn human life. Let this conversation be one based on the truths of love and not on the harsh accusations or judgments of the past. Let's have a conversation not based on the fickleness of a superficial emotional love that comes and goes but on that spiritual love that we all possess deep inside—the love where we say, *"Your life is more important than mine. I will protect you as long as I live, especially within the womb."* Let us bring this type of love to all pregnant women and to the life of the unborn child she has inside of her. Let us have a conversation where the respect that women deserve for their unique ability to bear children is restored and makes right again the integrity and responsibility of men in caring for both the pregnant woman and child.

This is the most important conversation we as a society can have today. Some of the most important voices in this new conversation will be the ones who once believed in the evils of abortion and now recognize and accept the truths of life and love. Who will be these important voices? Who will admit that they once bought into the evil lies and deceptions of abortion but now see truth? Who will be the politicians, actors, news anchors, business leaders, entertainers, and anyone else with a public platform who once desecrated the dignity of unborn life and used their positions to spew proclamations calling for their brutal destruction to stand up and say, "I was wrong," and publicly fight for the life of the unborn baby?

Who will come out from the comfort of the middle or have the courage to act upon their pro-life position and in a loving, respectful manner lead others to the truth and beauty of unborn life and the womanhood of those who support it for nine months? Who will be that beautiful person who, through courage and love with the knowledge of truth in their hearts, will work to transform our culture of death and disposable life into a culture of life and love?

There will be challenges. But if we focus on love, again the kind of love where we place the lives of others in front of our own, each one of these challenges will be met with success.

Of course, there will be those who still insist on promoting a pro-abortion position. In this new conversation of life, however, they cannot hide their excuses and justifications for abortion behind deception, lies, and the avoidance of fact. Instead, they must be made known of the truth. Then they must be asked, *Why?* Why do they insist that the intentional killing of an innocent living unborn human child is responsible, moral, and should remain legal? By asking why, we will quickly find out the real evil intents behind legalized abortion. But this will be a discussion for another day.

And in addition to asking why, pro-abortion government officials must also be forced to answer *How?* How can the "life" of an unborn baby, confirmed as *living* and then *killed* in the legal definition of abortion, at the same time be claimed as just a *potential* life within the law in order to justify the legalization of abortion in the first place?

This new conversation will be a conversation of truth. You now know truth. With truth, there is no need to be afraid to defend the life of an unborn baby or to stand for the true dignity and respect of a pregnant woman. There are no question marks when it comes to unborn life and absolutely no question on the realities of abortion. You know that life is recognized and acknowledged in science, medicine, and within United States law to begin at the moment of conception. You know that the very definition of abortion states that the living unborn baby must be killed before being removed from its mother.

Only truth will set us free from the evils of abortion. And with the victory of truth and love, we will find what has been lost for so long in the hearts of today's society—ultimate peace.

This is now up to you. You have been called. The very most important voice in this conversation is yours.

The next time you find yourself confronted with conversation regarding abortion, a conversation that is hostile to unborn children and degrades the dignity and respect of a pregnant woman, you have nothing to fear. Simply nod your head, smile, and then with love in your heart and truth in your mind—

Change the Conversation.

I thank God for

the inspiration and insight to write this book.

And for

the logic of my father,

the compassion of my mother,

my siblings, each individual, one family,

my wife who is always, always there for me,

my children who are so loving,

my friends who are so willing to help,

and for all the prayers everyone has prayed on my behalf.

But most of all I thank God for life,

for when there is no life

there is only emptiness.